MW01103753

CHERISHED INTIMACY

BRENTON and MARGARET YORGASON

Library of Congress Cataloging-in-Publication Data

Yorgason, Brenton G., 1945-
    Cherished Intimacy / by Brenton G. and Margaret Yorgason

ISBN 0-9667480-5-0

Printed in the United States of America

10   9   8   7   6   5   4   3   2   1

CONTENTS

PART ONE

Foundations of Intimacy

1

Of One Heart

> *Marriage enlarges the scene of our happiness and of our miseries. A marriage of love is pleasant, of interest, easy, and where both meet, happy. A happy marriage has in it all the pleasures of friendship, all the enjoyments of sense and reason, and, indeed, all the sweets of life.*
>
> **Addison**

INTRODUCTION

Our past three decades together have been filled with magic. We have had challenges, but these have brought us closer as we have worked through them. While at times stumbling in our efforts to strengthen the bond of intimacy, we have experienced many more moments of resounding joy.

1

Much of our pivotal learning comes from our religious values. Our orientation is the Judaic/Christian tradition, and we have invited the Savior into our home as we have reared our family. We believe spiritual intimacy is one of the vital facets of a happy marriage. We now invite you, independent of your religious persuasion, to examine our concepts and principles from your own perspective. We learned them through experience, both in the trenches and from the mountain heights. We supplement and confirm our experience with scientific research.

This information will help many young couples as they begin their journey together, as well as seasoned travelers as they continue along this path.

For Singles and Marrieds Alike

We have not written this book *solely* for married people. We have many friends and loved ones, who are not with the companion of their dreams. They have either never married, have married and are now divorced, or have experienced the death of their partner. These single adults can and *do* experience facets of intimacy while waiting for marriage to enjoy the sexual expression.

Intimacy Defined

Intimacy is unity or oneness—in mind, body, and spirit—experienced by a man and woman for the purpose of making the relationship last.

We chose the two words *Cherished Intimacy* for the title of this book because of their combination of strength and connectedness. They convey a sense of belonging and singleness of purpose.

Considered separately, **to be cherished** implies something that goes above and beyond love. A popular song goes something like this: 'Cherish is the word that I use to describe. . .the feelings that I have hiding here for you inside'. Webster defines cherish as 'to hold dear, to feel or show love for'. It comes from the Latin root word *carus,* meaning dear or valued, and includes the foundational concept of charity. In Christianity, charity is "the pure love of Christ." It is the act of reaching out, lifting another, and desiring to meet their needs.

Intimacy, by contrast, is a basic human need. We crave intimacy. Just as food, water, clothing, and shelter are vital for survival and growth, intimacy is necessary for emotional development. Human beings have a need for familiarity and closeness in associations, and intimacy is one of the core elements that fulfills this need.

Diamonds Are Brilliant and Enduring

Like a brilliant diamond, intimacy is multi-faceted and can be examined from many perspectives. Its greatest brilliance and luster can best be enjoyed when surrounded by the utmost light.

Margaret states: "Ever since our college days when Brent began selling diamonds part-time, he has had a fascination with this beautiful stone. He purchased a diamond wholesale and eventually slipped it onto my finger the night we became engaged. While he insists that I may have been a bit blinded by the glitter of that nearly flawless gem—since I quickly accepted the gift as a commitment from *my man*—I accepted it eagerly!"

Brent adds: "What Margaret might be remembering is her love for diamonds, and not for a smooth-talking country boy. Since that night we have contemplated the beauty of the diamond and how much we enjoyed turning it in the light."

Just as that diamond is multi-faceted and nearly flawless, a marriage can become such. Even as diamonds are the consequences of pressure and heat, so are intimate marriages.

Once a diamond is formed, it becomes nearly impenetrable. Likewise, if a couple can achieve marital intimacy, very few outside forces can chip or shatter the gem.

This Book's Power

The three-fold purpose of this book is to examine the foundation stones of intimacy, the potential eroding elements of this foundation, and the compelling brilliance of the many facets of intimacy.

While we come to this project with trepidation, we are on a quest for truth. Rearing a family has tempered our ideals, and a rigorous practicality has emerged.

Brent adds to the legacy of the first diamond he purchased. "Several years ago, Margaret gave her diamond to our son, Aaron, who was smitten with a beautiful young lady named Susan. Aaron's intent was to give this diamond to Susan when they became engaged. This mission was accomplished. They were later married; and now, as parents of a beautiful baby daughter, they are discovering more and more facets of intimacy in *their* marriage. The diamond on Susan's left hand reflects in the sunlight and seems to shine more brightly now than it did when I purchased it for the girl of *my* dreams."

Our Central Theme

We now pass along to you principles of intimacy so that you can more fully enjoy *your* intimate relationships. Benjamin Franklin said that "time is the stuff life is made of." We suggest that intimacy—true oneness—is the stuff a lasting relationship is made of. There is no substitute.

An Introductory Caution

The sexual scripts of intimate relationships are varied and of a very personal nature. We place many of them on the table for examination; however, as authors we feel that wise couples refrain from discussing their intimate relations with others—other than professional therapists, or ecclesiastical leaders, when one of the partners feels dissatisfied.

Romantic Love—A Prelude

Creating intimacy is a process, not an event. A couple passes milestones as they are falling in love—perhaps more correctly—*growing* in love. This process includes romantic love.

There are many couples, especially those who have been married for a long time, who think romantic love is superficial. This is not true. Romantic love is a prelude to a lasting love. It is doubtful that a couple is capable of feeling more than romantic love at the time of marriage. Physical attraction, attended by ringing bells and twitterpated hearts, is the fuel that ignites the fire of love that burns down to become the coals and ambers of a sustained glow. These coals and ambers can endure year after year—constant and warm, and even intensifying in heat and light.

While romantic love is a prelude to lasting love, it can be easily confused with *false* loves that can undermine permanent relationships. These false loves are:
> (1) falling in love with love,
> (2) falling in love with being loved, and
> (3) infatuation.

The first two of these are self-explanatory. Infatuation, however, resembles romantic love—but only at first glance. Infatuation tends to be more frequent among young adolescents in their early teens. It tends to last a short time, and often takes place soon after a previous involvement has ended.

Romantic love, however, brings new energy and ambition in life, leads to a deeper love, and is accompanied by kindlier feelings toward others in general. Unlike infatuation, it usually takes root slowly, and grows with time.

For purposes of this discussion, romantic love leads to a lasting love, but is not left behind. It continues as intimacy deepens.

5

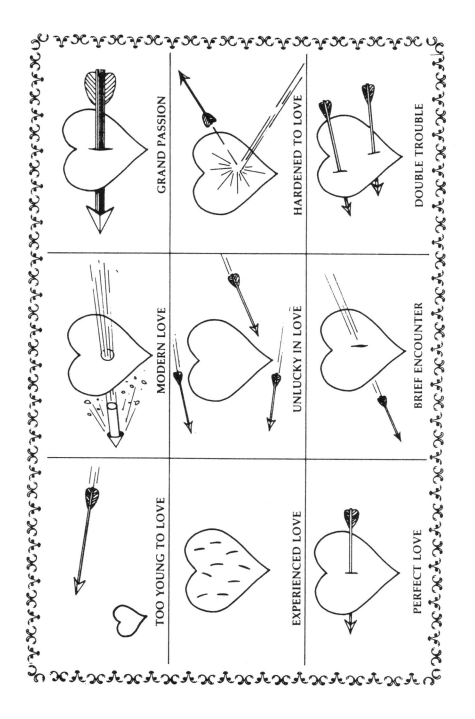

GRAND PASSION

HARDENED TO LOVE

DOUBLE TROUBLE

MODERN LOVE

UNLUCKY IN LOVE

BRIEF ENCOUNTER

TOO YOUNG TO LOVE

EXPERIENCED LOVE

PERFECT LOVE

> *When you sit with a nice girl for two hours, you think it's only a minute. But when you sit on a hot stove for a minute, you think it's two hours. That's relativity.*
> **Albert Einstein**

Lasting Love

All true love is founded on sensitivity, trust, respect, and concern for your partner. In all respects, your concern should equal your concern for your self.

Once this foundation is laid, caring enables a couple to express their deepening feelings. It allows them to deepen their sexual, emotional, and spiritual expressions. In turn, these expressions create and sustain a couple's unity.

Realistically, the frequency of tender utterances abate during the years of child-rearing. This is natural. Fortunately, greater focus and energy can be given once the children leave the nest. Couples experience rejuvenation that remains for life.

Keep Fanning the Fires

We have found that those couples who continue to court succeed at keeping the fires of romance burning better than those who submit to reality. Consistent courting is a proven method of nurturing intimacy. This includes a dating schedule, a light-your-fire mentality, and continual romantic gestures.

Couples of one heart share every aspect of their lives. They are concerned and want to know at the end of the day what their spouse did that day, and how she or he is feeling about life in general. Even though they have separate experiences and interests, they long to be with each other.

With this in mind, a wife who is not a sports fan will attend a ball game with her husband. She is not only rooting for his team, but is cheering for him. Likewise, a husband can develop his cultural side by taking his wife to an orchestra performance that she really wants to attend. A couple's varied interests may separate them at times, but by periodically sharing activities, they can be drawn together.

Lasting Love Invites Charity

From ancient Christians, especially the apostle Paul, we learn that charity involves three central themes. These are (1) that we should be more concerned about our partner than ourselves; (2) that we should be patient with ourselves, as well as with our partner; and (3) that we should be pure in our desires as well as in the way we treat our partner.

As mentioned above, deeper than romantic love is concern that focuses primarily on the needs and desires of our partner. Marriages in which partners focus on themselves, are those with the superficial and erosion-prone foundation of SELFISHNESS. When selfishness exists, partners compete with each other, rather than cooperate, while their needs for intimacy go unfulfilled.

A friend explains it this way:

I think that our ideas of what love is change with the passing of time. I have found that love is being able to place someone else's feelings, comforts, and needs above my own. When I have given that kind of love and support unselfishly, I have been able to realize that I also helped myself, even though at the time I didn't think I was. At the time I thought I wanted something else for myself.

The most difficult thing my husband and I have ever had to deal with was having our precious daughter killed in a highway accident. We both felt that we had been scalded to our very souls; we were hurt as deeply as it will ever be possible to be hurt.

When it happened I just wanted to go to my bedroom; go to bed and lie there alone in the dark and die as soon as possible. But I had to think of my husband and our remaining son. He was eleven years old at the time, just six years younger than his sister, and had enjoyed a remarkably close relationship with her.

For months afterwards, I had to force myself to get up and get dressed, put on some makeup, clean the house, and talk about something else. I fixed the meals as I always had. I walked and talked while I was dying inside. I never had it off my mind more than thirty seconds, yet I knew if I failed my husband and son at that point, it might ruin our family and make it much harder for them.

I am sure that for my own welfare it was best that I kept moving and working and trying to find something else to talk about with the two remaining members of my family. I know that if I had not had them, I would have given up and perhaps died or gone insane, and so I now see that I really helped myself by loving them so much that I put them first. Little did I realize that they were both doing the same for me. As a result, we all learned that truly loving someone is giving of oneself and caring first for the welfare of another.

This type of charitable love, even in the face of extreme hardship, welded this family unit together. This woman displayed maturity which helped both her husband and their remaining child. It takes courage to look beyond one's self. Such maturity is closely linked with charity.

The Precious Gift of Humility

When two individuals first wed, there is nearly always an obvious effort by both to care for their partner. Selfishness is nowhere to be found. For all too many, however, the honeymoon fades quickly. People revert to old habits like finding fault and criticizing. These are the sure-fire symptoms of pride.

> *Sense shines with a double luster when it is set in humility. An able and yet humble man is a jewel worth a kingdom.*
>
> **William Penn**

When married partners remain humble, they foster other qualities. Among these are:

- The desire to serve
- A soft and gentle nature
- The propensity to be honest
- A willingness to listen, then adjust
- The ability to compromise, even when right
- A desire to share feelings, for it is safe to do so

The Gift of Patience

Happy is the person whose partner has developed patience! Such a person is not easily provoked to anger. They have peace-filled thoughts, even when difficulties arise. They are quick to forgive and forget when their partner behaves selfishly. They bear burdens that are not theirs.

> *Patience! Why, it is the soul of peace. Of all the virtues, it is nearest kin to heaven. It makes men look like gods.*
>
> **Decker**

10

All lasting relationships are a result of patient collaboration. This involves varying degrees of suffering. Suffering, if borne with patience, produces growth. But to suffer does not mean to merely endure. According to Webster, it means "to allow; permit; tolerate." If you want to nurture intimacy, the cost is suffering. Patience enables you to pay the price without becoming resentful.

Expressing Thanks

As two people court, they consciously seek behaviors that the other will find attractive. One behavior is especially effective—constantly expressing gratitude for your partner's kindness. One of our dearest friends, Sheila, shares of her husband:

> *One of the thoughtful things David does is to constantly tell me of his love and appreciation. He tells me he loves me every day.*
>
> *David has never forgotten to thank me for fixing his meal, even when it's been a sandwich and a glass of milk. With that kind of thoughtfulness, he rarely gets just a sandwich. I feel like he deserves the best, so whatever it is, I try to make it very special. After all, what I do will be appreciated because he tells me so!*

CONCLUSION

Being "of one heart" is the goal of every couple as they fall in love. Two hearts begin to beat as one, creating an invigorating rhythm. Couples feel physical attraction to each other when this happens. They experience romantic love that is invigorating and purposeful. Romantic love, if nurtured, deepens into meaningful, charitable love. Charity can be detected in yourself if you exercise humility and patience in your intimate relationship. You reinforce intimacy and quietly invite your partner to do the same by expressing gratitude. Finally, charity is the sure foundation on which a lasting marriage is built.

2
Becoming Authentic

Captivating with Kindness

The lasting impact of charitable acts of kindness cannot be overstated. These acts become deposits in an emotional investment account, security against the difficulties ahead. Recent research has underscored the benefits of being kind within the family. Kindness invites trust, sharing, and love. Kindness also provides direct benefits. It fills the mind and heart with peace, which in turn stabilizes character in the face of relentless change.

> *The best portion of a good man's life is his little,*
> *nameless, unremembered acts of kindness and of love.*
> **Wordsworth**

Eliminating Uncharitable Acts

As effective as charitable service is, it is not adequate by itself to foster intimacy. You must eliminate uncharitable acts. This can be tough. Uncharitable acts are often habits you no longer control: angry outbursts, a scornful tone of voice, a disdainful facial expression. You must become master of your bad habits by changing them. You do this by teaching yourself to respond differently when difficult moments arise. Otherwise, you become a hypocrite, preaching but not practicing.

Rituals of Love

A sure way of deepening intimacy is to observe rituals. These rituals include remembering and honoring each other's birthdays, anniversaries, Mother's and Father's Day, Christmas, Valentine's Day, and other special occasions. Doing something special for your partner on these days allows them to feel loved, and gives you added assurance as well.

It is wise to avoid the trap of measuring love with money. One friend received a Valentine's Day letter that his wife crafted by hand, and gave us permission to share it:

14

DECLARATION OF LOVE
Valentine's Day

*Be it known unto all the world and the inhabitants of this
family that I dearly love Stan.
Not only on this given day of love, but for all time and
beyond.
Hereby signed and sealed with an holy kiss —*

Love — Barbara

This declaration was written on parchment and sealed with a lipstick kiss. Stan taped the scroll to the wall above his computer, just below his favorite photo of Barbara. He never tires of reading it.

Margaret concludes this topic with a thought that puts this ritual, along with others, into proper perspective:

"I not only enjoy doing things for Brent, but I appreciate his acts of kindness in return. There is nothing that enters a woman's heart so quickly as a token—like an unexpected phone call in the middle of the day—that lets her know she is treasured by her lover and sweetheart. It makes the day brighter, and infuses energy into her own desire to remember him. Just as well-prepared food is the best way to a man's heart, so are well-prepared rituals the best way to a woman's heart!"

Feeling a need for equal time, Brent adds: "While I deeply appreciate Margaret's expression of what I do for her, these acts pale in comparison to what she does for me. Even though she spends her days orchestrating a very complex home and family system, still she remains aware of my needs. I'm not even close to being that sensitive when it comes to serving her."

Serving Your Partner As Your Theme

A *theme* is an idea so important that it is repeated over and over. If you make "serving your partner" your theme and your priority, you will achieve intimacy.

Almost always, a woman has a more natural inclination toward nurturing than does her husband. In too many relationships, both partners have the same person as their theme—the man! This pattern does not need to perpetuate itself, however. As time passes, both partners need to feel cherished—to feel like they are each other's *theme*. While women serve more naturally, men need to follow suit and consider their partner's needs over their own.

On a recent flight to Portland, Brent sat next to two very special ladies—Julie and Susan. They were returning from a convention in Atlanta, and were in good spirits. When Brent pressed them in conversation to learn why they were so giddy, Julie blurted, "Because we're not with our husbands!"

This comment elicited conversation, and before long both Julie and Susan were revealing a lack of joy in their respective relationships. Inquiring further, Brent asked them what they each wanted from their husbands. Julie exclaimed, "To be respected!" Susan quickly added, "To be cherished!" These comments reflected reality, and while both of these women were committed to making their marriages work, each revealed a lack of intimacy and warmth—and neither seemed to have a husband who had *them* as his theme!

Sadly, society communicates that a *real* man's theme is sports. A real man's priority is to play sports when young, and to be an avid spectator after he stops playing. However, those rare men who put their partners first see miracles happen. They lead fuller, richer lives. So do their partners.

A man can put his partner first by washing her car, vacuuming the floor, and running errands *before* he tries to meet his own needs. Of all the principles in this book, making your partner your theme is one of the very most important.

Character Paradigm of Intimacy

During his years of counseling and teaching Family Science courses at a university, Brent developed a model for intimacy. This model suggests that if couples want to experience joy, they must labor together to build a structure that can sustain it. Removal of any of the building blocks in the structure causes the whole thing to collapse.

As you examine this model, do so with the understanding that *character* is defined as internalized moral strength—the ability to sustain a decision long after the emotion of making the decision has passed. It encompasses the entire model, and is a prerequisite to its components.

PARADIGM
OF
CHARACTERED INTIMACY

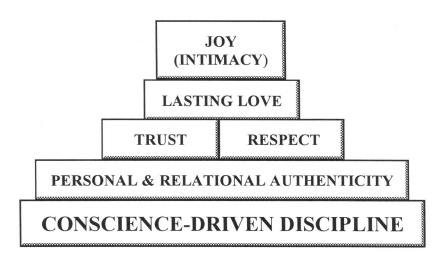

Components of Character

Conscience-driven discipline is the willpower to make correct choices. These choices are made because of an "inner voice," or conscience, that encourages goodness. For Christians, the desire to be good is called having the light of Christ. For others, it is the propensity to be good. It is the foundation necessary for authenticity, or integrity, to exist.

Personal authenticity, or being true to one's values, can include things like abstaining from Internet pornography, being truthful in business, filing an accurate tax return, etc. This type of authenticity is private, yet ripples out to impact every part of life.

Relational authenticity, by contrast, is a person's commitment to be true to their partner. This includes refraining from flirting, dating, and other illicit activities. One has but to look at Bill Clinton's agony to perceive the consequences of relational inauthenticity.

Having these authenticity building blocks in place allows for *trust* and *mutual respect* to emerge, which in turn enables *love*. The structure, or process, culminates in intimacy and joy.

Joining Two Different Scripts

As a person matures, they accumulate habits—ways to become comfortable in doing things. These accumulations of habits and biases are **scripts**. There is one script per person. Among the many habits comprising a script include the manner of handling one's finances, the ways they interact with a partner, the way they define sexual intimacy, and so forth.

Two people forming a permanent relationship must find a way to blend their scripts. Merging scripts usually occurs unconsciously. Making them conscious can help a couple spot and solve points of conflict. During problem-solving, a person cannot assume their script is more important than their partner's. The scripts are blended with accommodation, compromise, empathy, and charity. Sometimes, a person must simply choose to *not* be selfish!

If a couple is truly in love, they will validate and sustain their partner's scripts where those scripts do not undermine the relationship.

Increasing Love through Service

We recently met a couple from California—Darryl and Susie Root. Darryl is in his second marriage, and is very much in love with his wife of three years. He shared a poem with us that he had written to Susie while they were dating. With their permission, we include the final verse:

Ode to Susie

I see a rose drink up the morning dew,
So thirsty, this breathtaking, striving flower.
I see you as this rose, and I the dew.
Drink of my love—
Thirst not, for I now have plenty.
Open your petals for all to see;
Show how beautiful you and I can be.

Reflecting on this beautiful expression of Darryl for his sweetheart, Susie, we see giving and receiving, and longing and believing. It is a statement that speaks volumes for how intimacy is achieved.

AND NOW, A NECESSARY TRANSITION

Reality intrudes in every intimate relationship. If you can spot the intrusions, you can better deal with them. The following chapter in Part Two discusses the flip side of marriage. It examines cancers that, if allowed to grow, eat away at the intimacy foundation of even the healthiest relationship.

As you read this chapter, use it to evaluate and discuss any negative trends in your relationship. Then correct your course so you both can regain the intimacy you once shared.

PART TWO

Eroding the Foundation

3
Marriage Meltdown

> *Anyone who imagines that bliss is normal is going to waste a lot of time running around shouting that he has been robbed. The fact is, most putts don't drop, most beef is tough, most children grow up to be just people, most jobs are often more dull than otherwise, and most successful marriages require a high degree of mutual toleration.*
>
> *Life is like an old-time rail journey—delays, side-tracks, smoke, dust cinders, and jolts. These are interspersed only occasionally with beautiful vistas and thrilling bursts of speed. The trick is to thank the Lord for letting you take the ride.*
>
> **Gordon B. Hinckley**

If two people are in love when they marry, and if both remain true to their shared values, there never needs to be a divorce. Without exception, each divorcing couple we have known well has fallen into at least one of these two categories. One or both partners were not in love, and/or one or both partners were untrue to their shared values. Frequently this is a small compromise, but it can also include a major moral betrayal. It can also include incurring unnecessary debt, dishonest business dealings, consuming illicit drugs or alcohol, or simply a change in personal, preferred lifestyle. Such a change might include a decline in faith which is manifest by no longer praying, not attending church services, or not living according to a couple's shared beliefs.

The Risk of Re-Writing History

The hazard—and tendency—of many who consider divorce is to re-write history, particularly their feelings toward their partner. More often than not, the person seeking divorce rationalizes the decision. They say, "I never loved him in the first place," or "She only enjoyed intimacy when I insisted." We could list endless such justifications; but that isn't necessary if you are aware of the blaming trap. Blaming usually spins a person out of control.

Cancerous Negative Lists

Any marriage partner can create a negative list long enough to justify divorce. It has been our experience that once a negative attitude about a person is locked in someone's mind, cancer begins to form. If this negative attitude is not appropriately dealt with, it will boil beneath the surface. When it accumulates enough negative energy, it will eventually boil over in rage, or hysteria, a state of being where intense emotion dictates one's behavior.

Disastrous Rage, or Hysteria

When negative lists first reveal themselves, they almost always do so in an emotionally-charged verbal exchange. In marriage, negative energy piles up until it triggers a physiological response. Blood pressure rises.

> *As couples, we should not try to resolve differences when hysterical, or upset.*

When blood pressure goes up, a person enters the emotion-filled state of hysteria. While everyone finds themselves in this state, at times, the danger rises when a person does so regularly. Once a pattern of getting upset is established, a person may become *chronically hysterical*—consumed with the spirit of anger.

Hysteria, or rage, affects things all the way down to the cellular level. Gradually the cells become accustomed to increased levels of adrenaline and hormones. Just as with drug and alcohol addictions, hysteria becomes easier and easier to enter.

> *Once a hysterical pattern is established in a relationship, it develops a hair trigger.*

Hysteria, or anger, begins to color how a person thinks about their partner and their marriage. This person begins to react to what their partner says and does with a certain fear and distrust. Once a person enters this negative state, judgmental thoughts and feelings pervade. If this pattern is allowed to progress into a chronic state, the relationship is in serious jeopardy.

In stable marriages, however, couples make so many deposits into the emotional bank account that when an unsettling moment takes place, it passes quickly and without long-term, negative consequences. Each partner sees the incident as isolated and short-lived, and not a part of the marriage fabric.

If you find yourself becoming frequently upset in your

relationship, change your response to what your partner may say. Instead of trying to get your word in to justify your position, make the time-out sign with your hands. Have this signal pre-arranged so that no offense will be taken by either of you. Then leave the room, allow a few moments for your blood pressure to return to its normal state, and return to discuss the conflict in a peace-filled environment. Be willing to talk, rather than simply giving the silent treatment.

The Error of Attributing Motives Falsely

Each of us makes an error at times in our lives. It is the error of wrongly attributing another person's motives to be selfish or impure. In marriage, we begin to assume that our partner says and does things for what they can selfishly *get* in the relationship, rather than for what they can give.

This condition takes place when past behavior of one partner is monitored by the other, then judged to be less than honorable. Suspicions arise, mistrust enters in, and the error of falsely attributing motives takes place. The partner who feels victimized then begins to make the even larger error of attributing selfish or impure motives to *all* their partner's behaviors.

With malice toward none; with charity for all. . .let us strive on to finish the work we are in.

Abraham Lincoln

The solution, although easily stated, is difficult to implement once a negative pattern has been established. This solution is to accept the statement or behavior of your partner at face value. It is true that trust and respect must be earned, but having a forgiving heart is also necessary if your relationship is going to prosper.

There are instances where one partner—usually the one who sees themselves as the victim—begins to assume the role of their spouse's conscience. Once this happens, a vertical relationship begins to form, and neither partner can indefinitely live in such a condition. Only an equal, bilateral relationship can last.

Viable marriages are those where the partners make a concerted effort to cut each other slack, and refrain from becoming judgmental when the other misfires. Marriage is the one relationship where partners must not assume the role of defining and directing the behavior of the other. This is not to say that honest exchanges shouldn't take place; they should. But blaming the situation, while leaving your partner's self-esteem intact, is the best remedy.

Four Degenerative Divorce Facilitators

John Gottman, in his book, *Why Marriages Succeed or Fail* (Simon & Schuster, New York, 1994, pp.72-97), discusses four stages that lead to relationship failure. Gottman refers to these stages as the "Four Horsemen of the Apocalypse." They are:

One: Moving from normal complaining to *criticizing*.

Two: Developing *contempt* toward a partner.

Three: Becoming *defensive* in verbal and non-verbal exchanges.

Four: Incorporating *stonewalling* techniques to protect one's self from a partner's wrath.

Let's examine these debilitating forces one at a time.

Stage One: From Complaining to Criticizing

Lodging an occasional complaint about one's partner is understandable—even desirable. No couple lives in a vacuum where each partner has all of their expectations met. Complaints help bridge the gap between expectations and reality.

Unfortunately, most couples do not stop at constructive

complaints. They begin to attack their partner personally. They belittle their spouse, attacking their personality rather than merely a specific behavior. Adding injury to insult, the attack usually blames the partner for the couple's suffering.

As Gottman says (p. 74), "trouble begins if you feel that your complaints go unheeded (or if you never clearly express them) and your spouse just repeats the offending habits. Over time, it becomes more and more likely that your complaints will pick up steam. With each successive complaint, you're likely to throw in your inventory of prior, unresolved grievances. Eventually you begin blaming your partner and being critical of his or her personality rather than of a specific deed. Or, if you have been stifling your complaints, they may one day explode in a barrage of criticism."

Stage Two: Moving from Being Critical to Having Contempt

Once criticism becomes the mode of interaction, partners become opponents. When this occurs, one partner (perhaps both) will begin to view themselves and their issues as the only relevant ones. They lose respect for their partner, and begin to establish a vertical relationship. No longer do they perceive themselves as being equal. They now see themselves as being superior, with greater insight, judgment and perspective. Contempt soon emerges.

Once vertical positioning occurs, the contemptuous partner will have full intent to insult and psychologically abuse their partner. As Gottman (pp. 80-81) points out, the following signs of contempt reveal themselves at this time:

1. Barbs, insults, and name-calling are thrown at the partner. These would include words such as jerk, wimp, fat, stupid, ugly, etc.

2. Humor becomes hostile. While on the surface quite clever, these public and/or private innuendos are very hurtful for the intended spouse, and further escalates the theme of contempt.

3. Mocking the partner when a compliment is extended.

4. Body language changes. Most obvious is the swift changes of the facial muscles. These include rolling the eyes, sneering, and curling the upper lip.

Stage Three: Defensiveness, the Swift Response to Contempt

As contempt becomes the order of the day, a couple will begin to respond to each other's contemptuous comments by becoming defensive. They now feel victimized, seeing their partner as the one at fault for the existing problem.

The following defensive patterns are evident in this third phase of marriage meltdown (Gottman, pp. 85-89):

1. Spouses begin to deny any responsibility, or blame, for what is transpiring.

2. When darts of blame are fired at a partner, that person makes the defensive maneuver of making excuses for what might have transpired.

3. Negative mind-reading is responded to with defensiveness. A partner begins to read their spouse's mind (or at least they *think* they do). This triggers defensiveness.

4. Cross-complaining. When a person is criticized, they totally ignore the comment, then lodge an immediate complaint of their own.

5. Rubber Man/Rubber Woman. In this pattern, a criticism bounces off the receiving partner by throwing the blame back to the initially criticizing spouse.

6. "Yes-Butting." In this pattern, a criticized spouse starts off by agreeing, then ends up disagreeing with what was originally said.

7. Repeating the Defensive Reply. When criticized, a spouse repeats their position again and again and again. While getting nowhere, this broken record reply is used often when arguing.

8. Whining. A reply focusing on *how* something is defended, rather than on the words, themselves.

9. Body Language. Whether shifting the body, the false smile, or folding the arms across the chest, this defense is very often used, and easily understood.

Stage Four: Stonewalling As a Last Resort

A person becomes exhausted by criticisms, contemptuous attacks, and responding defensively. When this happens, they eventually stop responding in *any* way to the accusing spouse. In essence, they build a wall of protection around themselves, steeling their mind and heart against the perceived threats.

When a couple reaches the point of stonewalling, it is often too late to save the relationship.

The hazard of making this statement is that all couples, at times, participate in stonewalling. It is when stonewalling becomes the chronic response that relationships seem irretrievable.

Couples finding themselves in this critical phase should make every effort to obtain professional help so that their marriage can be saved.

Additional Issues to Consider

Carrying Guilt without Cause

More often than not, a person is their own worst critic. When something in life goes bad—and it most assuredly will if one lives long enough—a person is wise to deal with it, then put it behind them. Often during these moments of misfiring—whether they be of a personal nature or within a relationship—the tendency is to carry unnecessary guilt from the experience, whether a person has been at fault, or not. Carrying guilt from the past limits a person's ability to experience intimacy in the present.

> *Although our minds do not have the capacity to directly change how we FEEL, we do have the capacity to change our THOUGHTS. Once this happens, our feelings change as a matter of course.*

While certainly accepting responsibility for what a person participates in, or has influence over, that person must learn to forgive themselves at the same time they forgive their partner. Because a person can't control their feelings about a given situation, they must learn to play mental tapes of forgiveness. That is, they change their *thoughts*. Once this is done, feelings change from guilt to resolution—from doubts and fears to hope and faith.

Losing the Will to Continue

Within a wounded marriage, couples often degenerate from *holy wedlock* to *unholy deadlock*. Once a couple sinks into the quagmire of a decaying relationship, they lose the will to continue investing in the relationship. Persons who give up at this point do so at great expense to their self-worth.

While there is a flood of short-term relationships in today's society, such early and often casual bailout is at times justified. Divorce is justified when (a) abuse is taking place, and will not stop, and/or (b) when one partner persists in violating the mutually shared values of the couple.

In considering an abusive marriage relationship, the victim should never allow a first-time occurrence to continue. Because of the power of the brain to transmit information through the nervous system to the cells, a habit can be learned (and remembered by the cells) by experiencing an event only one time. It does not take repeated abusive experiences for an abusing spouse to "develop a habit" to repeat such abuse. This is why physical abuse, once administered, is so much easier to repeat—and is repeated with increasingly harmless issues.

CONCLUSION

The agonizing process of observing a once thriving marriage spin out of control is becoming all too common. More and more, we are living in an easy in/easy out marriage society. As authors—and as one couple who understands the perils and pitfalls of parenting, marriage, and life—we suggest that divorce need never take place.

This sweeping statement is made on the premise that repenting and forgiving can occur. Even more severe, abusive and controlling behaviors, as well as violations of the marriage vows, can be worked through and made whole. Humility, a desire to change, and a forgiving spouse, all factor in to the equation of saving a marriage in peril.

Reconsider marital issues you may have swept under the rug and left unattended. These issues, while not easy to detect beneath the rug, can become an agitating clump of dirt that scars the marital floor.

If you are struggling in any of the areas discussed in this chapter, seek help! You don't have to live in an abusive, destructive marriage. Change can and does take place in struggling homes, and in counseling centers, every day of the year. Unconditional love and forgiveness can occur when an errant partner chooses to humble themselves and seek help. A MARRIAGE *CAN* RESTORE ITSELF!

PART THREE

Facets of Intimacy

4
Verbal Intimacy

> *Wise sayings often fall on barren ground;*
> *but a kind word is never thrown away.*
> **Sir Arthur Helps**

A Trip into Yesteryear

In beginning Part Three, we invite you to sit back and relax, and take a journey into eighteenth century western America. It proves a point as well as provides a rest from the myriad concepts shared in the last chapter. Enjoy!

The time is the late 1800s, the place is a newly constructed meetinghouse in the newly-populated western frontier village, Fort Ephraim. The setting is the wedding ceremony for two young Swedish immigrants performed by an aged minister who barely speaks English, but who is doing his best to capture the appropriate spirit for this occasion.

"Ladies undt gentlemen. . . ."

His plow-calloused hands caressing the white pine finish of the new pulpit, the minister surveyed the congregation with satisfaction and pride. Even to the three-sided galleries, the new meetinghouse was filled to overflowing.

Since 1854, Fort Ephraim had protected the colonizers. Its inhabitants—men, women, children, dugouts, covered wagons, corrals, chicken coops, chickens, a church and a school, were walled up in a rock enclosure. At night, flocks and herds were driven into the fort for protection.

Having made their first excursions out of the protection of the fort to build this house of worship, the people were grateful to have what seemed an oasis for body and soul.

Here it was that the great events of life were celebrated. Today the congregation had gathered for a wedding, and if the English language suffered a few casualties with the Scandinavian minister, worse things had happened.

"Ladies undt gentlemen," the reverend began, "Ve air accumulated here today to behold von of da most sacred ordinances it is within our power to do. Ve has before us da vedding ceremony of Yon Yacob Yorgensen and Helena Sophina Turkelsen. . . .

"You young people up dere in the gallery!" the minister suddenly interrupted. "You vill please to produce no noise!

"Now," he resumed, "if da congregation vill please come to attention, Yon Yacob and Helena Sophina, you vill please come up here to dis pulpit."

"Now, Yon Yacob Yorgensen, please take Helena Sophina Turkelsen by da right hand. No, not shake hands, yust hold hands!

"So now," he continued, "before dis congregation, and before all da holy angels, do you Yon Yacob take Helena Sophina for your vife? Do you promise dat you vill be a good, kind, loving and attentive husband? You say you vill?

"Ladies undt gentlemen, he say he vill.

"And now, Helena Sophina Turkelsen. . .yust keep hold of da hand! Do you promise dat you vill take Yon Yacob Yorgensen for your husband and dat you vill be a good, kind, and loving vife vhen he is sick, vell or hard to get along vith? You say you vill? Ladies undt gentlemen, she say she vill.

"So now, if dere is anyone in dis congregation dat has any obyections to dis ceremony, vill you now speak up or forever shut up and mind your own business?"

Looking around, the minister was relieved that no protestations had been made.

"Dere being no obyections," he continued, "so now do I, da duly constituted minister, before dis congregation and before da holy angels—undt vith all da authority I has under my vest—pronounce you father and mother". (True account adapted from Grace Johnson account in the Fort Ephraim Messenger-Enterprise, Inc., 1973, pp. 32-33.)

———————

It is probable that these instructions were the only ones given to these young newlyweds. It is likely too that, after a day or so honeymooning, this couple began to toil sixteen to eighteen hours a day in an attempt to support their new family. It is also conceivable that over the years they fell into the habit of seldom articulating their feelings about their marriage, let alone reading and learning how to improve their relationship with each other.

Evolving into a High-Expectations Society

Much has taken place during the hundred-plus years since this couple was naively pronounced "father and mother"—and within the passing of these years a society has evolved wherein couples can and ofttimes must talk about aspects of marriage as well as their expectations about achieving true intimacy with their partner.

Contrast the standard marriage beginnings of yesteryear with the thoughts shared by a modern woman. She reflects on her experience with marital intimacy and the crucial role of sharing feelings and expectations:

There are several reasons why our marriage, as well as the quality within our marriage, is so good. The first is that we have been open in talking about our feelings, frustrations, what we like and don't like, etc. At first it was not easy for me to be so open; but through continually trying, patience, understanding, and time, it has become easier. Now, after almost thirty years, it is just second nature to me.

Another reason is that my dear husband has always, without exception, been very thoughtful about my feelings. From our first night together, he has let my feelings be the determining factor; and from that first night I have felt that I could honestly express my feelings. Because he has been so thoughtful of me, it has created a healthy cycle. I try harder to please him, and he tries harder to be considerate of me. The sexual part of our marriage has perpetuated itself, so to speak, because of our desire to please and help each other.

A third reason we have had such success is because of a little gimmick we adopted somewhere along the line which we call "donation." If I'm not as interested in closeness, then I can be as passive as I feel like being during our moment of intimacy—and this response (or lack of it) doesn't create threatening feelings inside of him. Often it can start out with me being passive, but it doesn't always end that way. Because of his gentle, loving manner, I end up being as involved as he is. And too, there are times when my husband is the passive partner, and where he responds to my needs for an intimate expression of my love for him.

While this example centers around physical intimacy, it also demonstrates the crucial nature of verbal intimacy—being able to effectively communicate with one's partner.

Another couple illustrates the importance of sharing feelings to increase the intimacy in their marriage:

Number one, we talk! We are very open about what we are feeling, both emotionally and physically. We have always tried to communicate in our marriage, and we feel it is vitally important. If we haven't had answers and solutions on our own, we have sought professional help from doctors and counselors. It is so important to try and keep all questions answered and problems worked out, and not to be afraid to seek outside advice, if such advice is necessary.

Number two, we are accommodating! Let us explain why this is important to us. Sometimes one of us is not in the mood to express love, however the other has a need to be fulfilled. This situation is not abused or taken unfair advantage of. It is important to fill the needs of our partners any way we can, whenever we can. It is also important for the partner in need to be understanding of the accommodating partner by realizing that this partner is giving unselfish love.

We have been married almost eighteen years, and we know our marriage will continue to grow because we both work at it.

Though Storms Arise

Two people can't hope to live together without experiencing *life*. Disappointments arise, bad decisions are made, children are infused into the family system, and differences occur. That is not the issue. The tragedy is that, when faced with inevitable difficulties, one or both partners too often choose to turn away from their vows and bolt from the relationship.

The following is one of our favorite poems, and sums up our feelings—including a poetic self-proclaimed justification for writing this book:

39

CLOUD NINE

Why is it
whenever I reach for the sky
to climb aboard cloud nine,
it evaporates and rains
upon my dreams?
Is it a matter of fact,
that not even a cloud
with a silver lining
can hold the weight of our dreams
without some precipitation?
I think I've found the answer
to this dilemma —
Keep on reaching for the sky,
but don't forget your umbrella.

Susan Stephenson

Indeed, all couples have "umbrella moments" in their marriages. Margaret remembers one such experience in ours:

In 1977, during the first semester of Brent's doctoral studies, he learned about the principle of "sharing feelings" within marriage. The idea of sharing feelings in a formal setting seemed risky to him, even though he was sure that our marriage did not need such mechanical instructions. After all, it had seemed almost perfect during the first ten years of our being together.

But as he left class that day, Brent decided he would carefully select a moment to check out my feelings about what he perceived to be a near-perfect relationship.

That evening, after our five children were successfully tucked in bed, he indicated that he wanted to have a special moment of sharing with me. We went into our family room, prepared a roaring fire in the fireplace, turned on the stereo, and then climbed confidently beneath the blanket on our sofa, each

40

unaware of the marvelous earth-shattering experience we would have in the next hour.

Taking me into his arms, Brent held me briefly and silently. Then, pulling back and looking into my eyes, he asked the question he had learned that day in class. "Honey," he whispered, "how do you *feel* about our marriage? Not what do you think about it, because I know that. I am interested in getting below the surface of your thoughts to explore your feelings about us."

For a brief moment I looked at him, my mind reeling with the impact of his question. I then did something that even I did not anticipate, something Brent had already learned was mine and every other woman's prerogative—to do the unexpected. I clouded up in about ten seconds and began to rain tears that turned into a torrential downpour. It is my memory (though it may not have happened exactly like this) that Brent got up, grabbed a bucket, and hurried and put it beneath my chin so the sofa would not become sopping wet.

About ten minutes later, after what had seemed an eternity, my tears gradually stopped. I then whispered my response.

"Brent, I'm so lonely! You are busy in your doctoral studies, with your community work, and in spending endless hours counseling others at the drop of a hat, not to mention the time you spend reading and watching sports on television. But I spend my life talking to children, doing dishes and loads of wash, and changing diapers. I just can't take it anymore. I need to know that you know I'm alive. I need you to *talk* to me!"

There, I had said it. Brent was stunned. I don't remember the balance of our conversation, except for the conclusion. Mustering strength, Brent announced the challenge his instructor had given to his class earlier that day.

"Margaret," he sighed, "why don't we set aside some time tomorrow night for sharing feelings? We can continue this routine for as long as we need to."

I smiled appreciatively, knowing how difficult it was for Brent to make such a commitment. I then agreed to his suggestion, and before I knew what was happening he whisked me off to bed and to my dreams.

Little did I understand the fear in Brent's heart. He had no idea what feelings we could talk about each night, even if it was for only a few minutes! For me, however, the prospect of getting to talk with him and actually share feelings each night gave me more optimism than I can now describe. I'll have to admit that I spent the next day wondering if we would actually follow through with our commitment to each other. I shouldn't have worried, however, for when 10:00 P.M. arrived, we were nestled under our electric blanket facing each other with anxious but determined smiles upon our faces.

That second sharing session was awkward, as was the third. Gradually, though, we found that our time of expressing feelings expanded to fill twenty minutes, then a full hour. We were both amazed at how much there was to talk about once the initial effort and commitment had been made. While our first conversations were limited and sometimes superficial, over time they became effortless and very pleasurable interchanges.

Brent remembers the events as they unfolded:

After a couple of weeks of our nightly conversations, we changed the rules. We determined that from then on we would respond to each other's desire to share feelings when the need arose. Because Margaret is usually the one with the need to share feelings and emotions, as opposed to my inclination to watch another game, to wash the car, to turn on the computer, to read another chapter in a book, or to just spend time with the kids, she is usually the one who initiates discussion.

If Margaret has such a need, she searches me out. The rule is that whatever I am doing, it is my responsibility to respond to her need to talk. Usually when she finds me, I notice a rain cloud gathering over her head, signaling her frame of mind.

Our agreement is that I stop whatever I am doing, make eye and body contact, and make every effort to really listen as she expresses her feelings. She then takes whatever time she needs, and if I have listened well I usually end the conversation by rescuing her from a home filled with overpowering children. I've found it absolutely amazing how much a little support and energy on my part smooths out her temporary waters of despair.

Margaret found that verbally sharing feelings led to other positive developments:

Even though both Brent and I are far from being perfect in this area, our ability to talk has increased immeasurably since that first rain-filled cloudburst. When we were newlyweds, we communicated quite well, but as children came along we found ourselves communicating less and less.

Falling into the vacuum of not speaking is a matter of natural course as a couple sets up housekeeping and the division of responsibility take place. Each partner becomes somewhat consumed by his or her roles. But feelings are the substance of a marriage, and if they are not shared a barrier is gradually created. Now, however, when we share regularly, I find that my feelings of frustration don't build up as they did before. I used to let them stay inside until I felt as though I would pop like a firecracker.

One of my favorite cartoons dealing with marriage is that of a wife glaring at her husband while he slouches in his easy chair, watching television. He states simply, *'I know we don't communicate. That's one of my few pleasures!'* I laugh at that cartoon now, but there are days in our marriage when I honestly feel like that lonely wife in the cartoon.

If I wait until I have a need to convey my feelings, then we've waited too long, and it is already too late! Feelings need to be expressed along life's highway, not waiting until we are dying of thirst before we take that refreshing drink.

Not long ago we shared this experience with some friends whose marriage has had difficult moments stemming from a very difficult beginning. Upon hearing of our "umbrella day," she said: "You talk as though a little rain is a downpour. For us, it has been one hurricane or cyclone or earthquake after another. Now, as we look back over twenty years of such massive storms of upheaval, we wonder if we have the energy or the ability to pick up the pieces."

We understand that, like ourselves, some couples only experience mild spring showers, while others weather torrential downpours. It is miraculous that this couple, as well as others like them, are still married. They have had many opportunities to be blown away by hurricanes and cyclones of conflict. If you are one of these couples, we commend you for weathering your storms and for being emotionally strong enough at this time to examine the quality of your marriage.

We have described a pivotal moment in our relationship with the hope that you will be encouraged to make a commitment to share your feelings with your companion. Perhaps reading and talking about the ideas presented in these pages will seem a bit too risky. But we believe that you will be pleasantly surprised at the results as you begin to really talk with each other and share feelings.

These days most of our talk time deals with thoughts and things that are happening all around us—everything from one child's dental appointment, to another's grades, to the frozen pipe in the kitchen, to the gas level in the car. Many of our conversations deal with the surface issues it takes to keep a family going.

These areas of family management are vital to keep a marriage running smoothly. But couples need to regularly dive below the surface and share on the feeling level. Emotions are such a vital part of life and of marriage. Without feelings, a marriage would be like a black-and-white television. On the other hand, sharing feelings brings color and depth to the marriage picture. While the process may sound easy, it can take a concerted effort to risk and to share, even with your closest friend, your marriage partner.

Each of us has brought different communicating techniques into marriage—skills or behavior patterns we likely learned by the example we had in our own homes as children. If your partner grew up in a home where his or her parents did not often express themselves, then you may feel as though you are pulling teeth to get a response from that partner. While it is hard for Brent to admit it, women are usually the "emotional managers" of a relationship. They are therefore the ones who find themselves pulling the teeth. Most men simply don't have the inclination to process a great deal of feelings. But they still have the need in order for the couple to be in touch and on the same emotional level.

Knowing When to Do What

Regarding the issue of timing, Margaret explains: "I have found that timing is a vital aspect of communicating. For instance, when Brent is watching a football game—especially if it is the San Francisco 49ers, I can be certain that he will not appreciate a deep sharing exchange with me. I try to be sensitive to the situation and wait for a better time to unload my heart."

Learning to label your emotions, or feelings, is a crucial skill that will allow you to be more expressive with your partner. You can acquire this skill by learning to identify your feelings, consider the words to describe them, and then share them with your partner.

Below is a list of feelings you can consider which will facilitate the verbal intimacy in your marriage. They are in the form of direct statements as well as metaphors:

DIRECT STATEMENTS
"I'm angry."
"I think I feel lonely tonight."
"I feel so excited that . . ."
"It is so depressing to . . ."
"I feel sad about. . ."
"Deep inside I have a feeling of. . ."

METAPHORS
"I feel like something the dog dragged in."
"I feel like I'm floating on a cloud."
"I feel like I'm carrying the whole world on my shoulders."

"I'm tingling all over."
"I feel like I'm ten feet tall."

Creating Understanding

In learning to verbalize feelings, the objective is for your partner to understand just what it is you are experiencing. One effective way to communicate is to use "I" statements. These are very different from "You" statements and "I-You" statements, and are especially helpful when expressing negative feelings where a partner is involved.

In the following three examples, consider how much better the "I" statements reflect a healthy marriage:

I statement: "I'm furious."
I-You statement: "I'm furious and it's your fault."
You statement: "You've made me furious."

I statement: "I'm so angry with this mess that I could scream!"
I-You statement: "I'm so mad at what you've done I could tear this place apart!"
You statement: "You've ruined the whole evening with this mess!"

I statement: "I feel as though I'm useless and unimportant."
I-You statement: "It hurts me when you don't come home on time or don't call."
You statement: "You don't even care about me, or how I feel."

It is obvious that the "I" statement has some strong advantages over the other forms of verbal expressions. It very clearly identifies your feelings, and it creates ownership. By using an "I" statement, you communicate that the feeling exists and that it is inside you. It is your feeling. The other great advantage of an "I" statement is that it shows that you accept the responsibility for the emotion.

For your partner, hearing you express an "I" statement leaves him or her undefensive and thus more able to learn about your feeling. That in turn helps him or her better respond to it.

One skill we, as a couple, have attempted to incorporate in our

46

marriage is that when one of us is upset, we try to separate our partner from the problem.

Margaret says: "Without wanting to appear ignorant, I've always had the notion that if I had three checks left in my register, that meant I had enough money to write out three more checks. Not often, but once in a while, this understanding has backfired. If Brent is upset with my overdrawn checkbook, he is careful to let me know that he is upset with the situation and is not angry with me. When my self-esteem is left intact, I can handle his comment without feeling defensive. It also allows him the opportunity to solve the problem by putting more money into my account. It works every time!"

While smiling at the above scenario, Brent is quick to reply: "Margaret has truly led out as the example in responding verbally to unsettling moments. She also allows my self-esteem to remain intact simply by blaming the situation rather than attacking me personally.

"An example of this took place not long ago when her car stopped, unannounced, and she had to walk several blocks home in a snowstorm. It was a 1951 Dodge, a restored throw-back to my first car in high school. She could have easily attacked me for not having the carburetor repaired, or for having to drive the antiquated car of my dreams. But she didn't. She simply announced that the Dodge was stalled on a certain corner. She then stated her frustration with not being home to have dinner ready, and said she would be happy to help me tow it down to the service station.

"At that moment I felt a sense of added security in my role of transportation provider, even though I had not done well in my stewardship."

On the surface, every person might consider it ideal if they lived in a world where only positive experiences and feelings existed. Such an environment would not be conducive to growth and progression, however. Each person must learn how to deal with difficult situations and then how to come to grips with negative experiences and feelings. Learning to verbally express these negative feelings can actually become an art. While most people will not gain Picasso-like perfection in their artistic endeavors, the following guidelines can assist in achieving verbal intimacy:

Guidelines for Dealing with Negative Feelings

1. Is the "total environment" right? Check out the time of day, distractions, noise, privacy, outside pressures in the home, and so forth. In other words, mentally strategize the appropriate time and place to express your feelings.

2. Ask yourself, "Am I in control?" Intense feelings may interfere with what your objective should be. Therefore, if you feel that you are too emotional to express your feelings, you may decide to privately vent your intense feelings first so that when you do express them to your partner, the results will be productive.

3. Ask yourself, "Is my partner in a mood to be receptive?" Is your spouse defensive, preoccupied, tired, or overworked? Preface your comments by asking: "Where are you now?" "Can I share a feeling?"

4. Remember: Be careful, sensitive, and slow. Use tact, love, and consideration as you share your feelings, and don't dump too much negative data at one time. If your partner becomes less receptive or defensive, wait until the proper mood can be recreated.

5. Be sure to include yourself in the problem. Almost all problems that cause intense negative feelings between partners are the result of interaction between them rather than from a single partner's actions. Use "I" statements. The resolution of your feelings will then almost magically take place.

6. Afterward, show an increase in love and tenderness.

Effective Listening

Until now in discussing the creation of verbal intimacy in marriage, we have concentrated on the role of the expressor, or the spouse who needs to share a feeling. An equally important skill in communicating with one's partner is that of receiving, or listening.

As an effective listener, a person must first have an attitude of attention and interest—an "I-care-about-what-you-are-about-to-say" attitude. Second, they must have a desire to listen with the ears, the mind, and the heart, so as to be able to comprehend what they are being told.

When a person listens with their mind and heart, they might first determine if they have heard what their partner is meaning to communicate. This can be done by asking something as simple as, "Do I hear you saying that you. . . ?"

Once a person receives a confirming signal that they are interpreting things correctly, it's much easier to resolve the issue at hand. But it is essential that a person provides verbal reinforcement to their partner.

Positive verbalizing, or paying compliments, can be the glue that holds a relationship together. While most spouses are quick to comment on the negative aspects of marriage, too often they take the positive things for granted. One author explains:

The best way one can help a tongue-tied spouse who does not communicate often, is by example. Compliments multiply and tend to beget other compliments. Nothing comes across phonier than false praise, so we must be sure to be sincere. On the other hand, many of us need to learn how to graciously accept a compliment with a sincere "Thank you," rather than with a contradiction. Telling our partner how much we appreciate them is a gift that costs nothing, yet means everything. Nothing says loving like sincere appreciation. (Diane Halles, "Words That Can Warm Up Your Marriage," *McCalls*, April 1989).

Let me be a little kinder, let me be a little blinder, to the faults of those around me. Let me praise a little more.

Edgar A. Guest

It is important to send as many positive verbal messages as possible. Verbal intimacy is achieved when a couple is successful at doing this as well as at sharing feelings of frustration, loneliness, and so forth. The underlying elements of such a relationship is mutual trust and respect, and only when these ingredients are present can a couple achieve true intimacy.

CONCLUSION

Words are more powerful than the sword. It takes two understanding hearts to truly share. Verbalizing thoughts and feelings is essential to a vibrant, growing relationship. It is perhaps the first type of intimacy a couple experiences as they prepare to become close in other areas.

Hopefully, the ideas explored in this chapter will become a springboard for you and your partner as you further refine your own skills of sharing and caring. Only then can you effectively internalize [and ultimately cherish] the other facets of intimacy, and thus prepare your relationship to stand the tests of time.

5
Nonverbal Intimacy

As one string upon another builds a rope
  to anchor the mightiest ship,
One loving act upon another builds ties that bind
  well beyond the grave.

Author Unknown

The Power of the Unspoken Word

Approximately eighty percent of all communicating is nonverbal. This statistic makes it clear that there is great power in unspoken messages. A thorough understanding of how to effectively send such messages in a positive way can lead to increased intimacy.

There are several kinds of nonverbal communication between couples, many having to do with touching, looking into one another's eyes, holding hands, and collapsing into each other's arms. These nonverbal signals will be discussed later. For now, there is another type of nonverbal communication that deserves discussion because it increases a couple's sense of oneness. It is simple kindness and sensitivity between a man and woman.

An Unexpected and Unlikely Beginning

In reflecting on the early days of our marriage, we both remember a very Camelot-like beginning. As two 22-year-olds, we innocently viewed marriage as a destination. Once we were married, we thought we had arrived. But we soon learned that marriage is much more like an exhilarating, though complex and hazardous journey.

Little did either of us realize, as we began our honeymoon, that five short months later Brent would be activated into the U.S. Army and would subsequently be sent to Vietnam.

That separation was a difficult one. We were just settling into a satisfying and rewarding marriage routine. In retrospect, however, it was a healthy separation. We found that by learning to express ourselves in letters, our love deepened and solidified. We found that writing feelings down on paper, where words were measured and chosen carefully, was a powerful exercise in learning to communicate effectively.

As we now reread those letters, we can see that it forced us to stretch ourselves and our communicating talents. We didn't just share thoughts and feelings, either; as time passed we found ourselves setting more and more goals, in ink. We now realize that this unexpected intrusion into our first year of marriage was most valuable for us in this respect. It allowed us to step back, evaluate our progress as a couple, and then recommit ourselves to the ideals upon which our marriage had been founded.

We believe that this forced nonverbal stretching early on served as a crucial anchor to our marriage.

Most couples don't have the experience of separating for a season while still floating along on the clouds of their honeymoon. Still, as a couple, you can begin today to enjoy fresh and invigorating air in your marriage by sharing feelings of love in a letter. Love notes are a treasure! Who doesn't relish the excitement of opening an envelope addressed to them to find tender words expressing love and appreciation?

Expressing feelings on paper is one way this intimacy can be achieved. A spouse could leave a note in their partner's lunch box, in their suitcase when they travel, under a pillow—or even deliver it to their place of employment. A working partner might write a letter to their spouse and mail it from work, or perhaps while on a business trip. E-mail is a great way to keep in constant touch!

If you are experiencing frustration or disappointment in your marriage, consider the possibility of writing down your feelings. This can be an effective way of expressing yourself, simply because you can choose your words carefully without having to give an immediate response.

Some marriage partners who are confronted with feelings of frustration find it much easier to express deep feelings on paper before talking things out with their spouse. From that point, a conversation on the subject is easier to approach. Some letters should never be mailed or given to a partner. If in question, seal it up, and keep it for a day or two, and re-read it to see if the message is too strong. Writing is good therapy for the mind, and is a good way to vent. Before you give it away, consider if it will do more damage than good.

There are two types of charitable acts that you can perform to better your relationship with your spouse. First, do things for your husband or wife, thus sending out a clear, romantic signal. These can be as direct as making your husband his favorite cake or leaving a mint on his pillow; or, for the husband, purchasing a new nightgown for your wife. Or they might be as indirect as polishing your partner's shoes or putting toothpaste on his or her toothbrush.

Sending flowers is a great way to communicate your love in a nonverbal way. Someone has said that the 'earth laughs in flowers.' Even though we all know they are perishable and won't last very long, the memory and fragrance will outlast the blossoms. It shows that you care, and it *is* the thought that counts.

Making the Load Lighter

The second type of charitable act involves a deeper commitment to intimacy than the first — and that is doing things that will lighten the burden of your partner's daily tasks.

A friend shares the feelings she has about her husband when he demonstrates this type of nonverbal intimacy: "Even without speaking, I have always appreciated how my husband lets me know he loves me. It might sound silly, but some of my most appreciative feelings surface during the middle of the night when he gets up and takes care of the baby. He doesn't always do this, but we take turns, and it lets me know just how much he loves me."

This woman's husband adds: "Never a moment passes in our home but what my wife is silently expressing her love, either to me or to one of the children. Whether it's preparing a meal, washing several batches of clothes during any given day, or simply bringing me a large glass of orange juice, which is my favorite.

"My wife's quiet messages of love seem to exact from me a desire to perform loving acts for her. My favorite is getting her car washed and then filling the tank with gas before I hand the keys back to her. Somehow these small acts of kindness do wonders for our marriage."

Still another woman, in reflecting her appreciation for nonverbal acts of love, states: "Adding to the luster of my diamond is my husband's increased involvement around the house. This has come about as he has become more aware of my needs. He has a personal goal for me never to have to pick up our vacuum, and he will sometimes even vacuum the family living area of our home twice a day. He'll employ the younger children to pick up ahead of him, and before I know what is happening, law and order have been restored to our home. His helping lets me know that he really does care about me."

However, if you say "I love you," but do nothing to support or show that love, then your actions are inconsistent with your words. Being sensitive to your spouse's needs, and then doing kind nonverbal deeds for your spouse, gives meaning to your words.

About the issue of a husband's involvement in keeping a home tidy and clean, Margaret explains: "I was recently given a book written by Don Aslett entitled *Who Says It's a Woman's Job to Clean?* In quoting from the *Wall Street Journal*, he states that women who are homemakers spend more than eight hours a day on house and family work, while women who are employed outside the home spend as much as five hours a day. This compares to husbands who spend only an average of thirty-six minutes per week in helping around the house.

"I don't share those statistics in a complaining way. I love being in my home, and I receive a lot of satisfaction from my full-time job as a homemaker. But I do begin to feel like a martyr if I am carrying the entire weight of the house on my shoulders. Husbands would be surprised at the great benefits of sharing the load.

"Again, Mr. Aslett states, 'Women become warm and playful when the house is clean, squared away, and running smoothly.' He then counsels husbands to 'take over some of the work and you'll have more time to play and be together. She'll be less irritated and naggy, prettier, a little more likely to believe that you really do care, and you can use your imagination from there. We'll really make all those macho foreign lovers sweat when we start making housework an all-American male passion.'

"I'm so glad my husband doesn't think of housework as 'your' job. He has taken *y* out of *your*, and has tried to make cleanliness in our home a team effort. This has given us a deeper meaning to our feelings as well as to our precious moments together."

Subtle Cues

There are other ways to communicate nonverbally, most of which couples don't realize they are using. These are more oriented to their interaction as a couple and include their tone of voice, facial expressions, body language—as well as the subtle, pervading moods they have as they interact with their spouse. In many ways, these nonverbal messages are even more important than the actual words expressed in conversation.

Even though physical closeness is a prelude to sexual intimacy, such closeness can be very fulfilling, independent of further intentions. Tender touching has profound power in any significant relationship. There is a closeness that comes from physically touching that can perform miracles, including healing misunderstandings and gaining a closeness and confidence that is crucial to a viable marriage. Many times the magic of touch brings great satisfaction and bonding to both partners.

As an example of the power of nonverbal intimacy, one woman shares: "Because of our busy lifestyle, my husband and I usually collapse in bed at the end of a day. We love to then catch our breath as we share the events of our day with each other. As we fall asleep, we cuddle up like two teddy bears, and continue to gain strength and reassurance from these hugs throughout the night."

She then becomes more specific: "I love my husband's hands! They are so rugged, yet so tender. I can recall vividly our first date when, for the first time, he reached over and took my hand in his. Now, years later, I love holding hands with him even more.

"In addition to the act of holding hands, I appreciate how my husband's hands show me so much love, with gentle caressing and expression. Then too, I love how his hands are helping hands and reach out to share the work. I also love how his hands bless my life. It makes me really believe that he truly loves me, because his hands actually prove it. My husband's hands show me that he loves me."

One woman shares a letter that she stuffed in her husband's shirt pocket:

My Dearest Husband:

How very much I appreciate your great tenderness with me. After having been away on a business trip and then returning home, you are so careful to be sure that I enjoy our intimacy. You treat me with such great respect. For me, I am best able to share myself with you after a day of small kindnesses from you —a hug, an expression of appreciation, a kiss after breakfast.

Even seeing you as a wonderful father increases my desire to be one with you—your delightful laughter as you help baby John with his first steps, your careful listening to our teenage daughter's concern over dating, and all the things you do with our other children. You see, I am able to love you so completely because you are such a good man in all areas of your life.

56

Perhaps I could say that the intimate part of our lives is not an event or a simple act—it is a complex part of the very fabric of our lives together.

Thank you for helping me look forward to our loving times by encouraging me, listening to me, appreciating me, and being so honest. I love you more than words can tell.

Yours forever

Sending Messages

Remember the cartoon mentioned in the previous chapter, "I know we don't communicate. . .it's one of my few pleasures!" This statement is actually false, for two people together cannot *not* communicate! They are always sending messages, whether it is with their tone of voice, gestures, facial expressions, or body language. Even the silent treatment says something.

If marriage partners do things with a wince and a grudge, feeling all the while as though they are being used, then their message will be loud and clear. On the other hand, if their attitude is one of service with love, it will be received in the same way. There is a universal law which states that "we love those individuals we serve."

Doing for others creates a bond. This is why parents love their children so much. They love them, not for all they have done for the parents, but for what the parents have invested in them. If this law is thought of as an equation that will work in marriage, a couple could say that service is a key to loving one another. Partners can learn to love their companions more as you do little things that please them.

It is good to verbalize nonverbal expectations and appreciations. Different people respond differently to nonverbal cues, and it is good to check out what one's partner enjoys or doesn't enjoy.

In *One Flesh, One Heart,* Dr. Carlfred Broderick gives examples of couples who appreciate such a tactic. He states:

I have known women who would melt if their husbands brought them an unexpected box of candy; I have known others

57

who would be offended that their husbands didn't support their attempt to cut down on sweets; and I have known still others who would feel that such a romantic gesture was a sly attempt to deflect their attention from the real issues in their relationship (whatever those might be).

Men are no easier to please. One might enjoy and appreciate his wife's help on a major project, while another would consider her meddlesome. Most men would probably appreciate their wives being more active in initiating sexual activity. Yet some would be offended, threatened, or put off by it. (Deseret Book, 1986, pp. 37-38.)

Dr. Broderick concludes with an intriguing question:

"Have you ever noticed that when couples give each other back rubs, they tend to give the rub they would like to receive rather than the one their partner wants? Thus a husband may give his wife a firm back rub that she finds painful and even intimidating, while she gives him a feathery massage that he finds ticklish and unsatisfactory."

The point is obvious. Individuals should feel so secure in their relationship with their spouse that they can verbalize what they like and dislike, in terms of nonverbal techniques and messages. Then, and only then, can a couple insure this type of intimacy in their marriage.

CONCLUSION

The intent of this chapter has been to provide insight into personal nonverbal cues that spouses can give each other to induce greater bonding and intimacy in their marriage. These stimuli occur when a couple interacts and sends nonverbal messages to each other, and when partners choose to perform acts of kindness for their spouse.

Hopefully, the ideas and personal experiences shared in these pages can assist you in reaching new nonverbal vistas in your marriage. This will occur spontaneously as you think of creative ways to nonverbally express your feelings for each other.

You can create further intimacy whether you have been married just a few short weeks, or whether you have washed each others' clothes and cars for several decades. Expressed consistently, these nonverbal techniques combine to create a bonding that, in turn, introduces an environment of profound trust and security between husband and wife.

6
Sexual Intimacy

> *Sex is as much psychological as physical. Certainly love is much more than physical sex appeal.*
>
> **Harold H. Titus**

On Higher Ground

The appropriate nature of the basic family unit of husband and wife is clearly and simply set forth in Genesis 2:24: "And they shall be one flesh." While today this is a common cliché, it is nonetheless important as we consider the binding and bonding that takes place as a couple does indeed become one flesh.

There is only one time when two individuals are truly one flesh. This, of course, is during the act of love, or procreation. During this act, two individuals become so personal and so intimate with each other that they actually become a part of each other. There seem to be at least two results of this personal, sacred moment of oneness. The first result is the deepening bond that is strengthened between lovers. The second result is the unique bond that develops between partners as a woman carries, and then delivers, a child.

The Potential for Exploitation

The challenge for each of us is to make proper use of our body, as well as our partners', by enjoying the moment of sexual intimacy without exploiting the other. In fact, as the two of us consider the singular experience of sexual intimacy, we honestly feel that one partner has the power to use this same moment to throw the relationship into a downward spiral, simply by exploiting the moment for selfish purposes.

As we will explain as the following chapters unfold, sexual intimacy is not an end in and of itself. Rather, it is a facilitator for emotional intimacy. As such, we should be cautioned against getting the intimacy emPHASis on the wrong syLABle. They regard sexual intimacy, and orgasm, as the ultimate benefit of the act.

The premise of this book, however, is that the physical union is an expression that provides an environment for increased emotional and spiritual intimacy. In fact, if these latter facets of intimacy are nonexistent, sexual intimacy begins to exploit and then ultimately contribute to contaminating a relationship. In particular, a woman must sense an emotional connection if she is not going to feel exploited. Feeling exploited occurs when the man gives her the feeling that he has his own selfish agenda in being intimate, and that he is focused on his own body and his pleasure; or on her body, rather than on her, as a person.

Lovemaking Is a Key to Marital Joy

Boyd K. Packer, a religious spokesman, has explained, "The experience of procreation is in fact the very key to our being truly happy." ("Why Stay Morally Clean," *Ensign*, July 1972, p. 113.) It is the way provided by God for his purposes of populating the earth.

According to Packer, the procreative power within each of us exhibits two significant features—it is both strong and constant. Knowing the difficulties encountered in rearing children, God has provided these features as a means of motivating us to have children. Without these features, many couples would be reluctant to accept the overwhelming responsibilities of parenthood.

Speaking further from a spiritual perspective, the Lord caused the experience of intimacy to be a bonding and unifying one for both men and women. Since this power of procreation is constant, it can serve as a medium for couples to develop, express, and foster delicate and intimate love feelings.

Contrary to much that is conveyed on the screen and in modern "enlightened" literature, the act of sexual intimacy is not intended to be a self-oriented, personal gratification experience. Rather, it is intended to be one where feelings of love, caring, and giving expand and grow within. As a marriage partner, you can no doubt appreciate that when two people have this orientation toward intimacy, they experience the highest and most noble feelings of love and companionship. Then and only then can two really become one and thereby share in the depth of purpose of this intimacy.

The Reverend Billy Graham has stated:

> The Bible makes plain that evil, when related to sex, means not the use of something inherently corrupt, but the misuse of something pure and good. It teaches clearly that sex can be a wonderful servant but a terrible master: that it can be a creative force more powerful than any other in fostering of love, companionship, happiness, or it can be the most destructive of all of life's forces. . . .
>
> God himself implanted the physical magnetism between the sexes for two reasons: for the propagation of the human race, and for the expression of that kind of love between man and wife that makes for true oneness. His command to the first man and woman to be "one flesh" was as important as his command to "be fruitful and multiply." ("Guidelines to Carry Forth the Work of God in Cleanliness," *Ensign*, May 1974, pp. 7-8.)

The premise of this chapter is that the sexual union is intended for both procreating and giving nourishment and strength to the marriage relationship.

Further Understanding

The sexual union has at times been thought of as a necessary obligation that should be tolerated, that it was the man's right and the woman's duty to repeat this experience. In recent decades, however, public views have changed dramatically.

The result has done more than correct the errors of the past. Like a pendulum swinging too far, society has moved into a period of excessive permissiveness, where sexual intimacy is flaunted and portrayed and abused to an almost unbelievable degree. This is no more clearly seen than in the much-discussed moral decay of America's leaders.

It is crucial to understand the appropriate, even God-given role sexual intimacy plays, and then stand firm in one's convictions rather than allow themselves to be influenced by what is portrayed on the Internet, on television and movie screens, or in magazines and books. As a society, we must avoid the extreme views of the Puritan and Victorian eras as well as the hedonistic extremes of our own sexually permissive day. Instead, we should seek after that which is appropriate and exhilarating.

As couples, we should seek after that which is uplifting and virtuous. This is true in the sacred area of intimacy in marriage as much as in any other part of life. The important thing to remember is that, as a people, we must sift the wheat from the chaff, retaining only that which is consistent with a stable value system. We should not only gather correct information about sexuality in marriage, but we should avoid or discard incorrect beliefs as well.

The Incomparable Human Body

Unfortunately, there are members of our society who have naively accepted the belief that the physical part of the body is evil and debasing and as such should be shunned and avoided. This belief dates back to ancient philosophies and continues to exist in several modern cultures. It springs from the concept that the mind or the spirit is the more superior part of man, while the physical body is the seat of evil things such as passions and corrupting influences.

This belief has led people to want to enhance the mental or spiritual parts, while avoiding or denouncing moments of physical fulfillment. From this orientation it is but a short step to defining the sexual part of man as primarily a part of the physical body rather than of the spirit. Thus this belief of labeling sexuality as being evil, carnal, and undesirable was incorporated into early Christian traditions and has unfortunately remained there for many people, even as we welcome the next century.

The view that the physical body is something low, and that sexuality in marriage is unholy or evil, is incompatible with revealed truths about the nature of man. The Holy Bible teaches that each of us is a temple (see I Corinthians 3:16-17), and that because the physical body was made in the image of God, it too is glorious and desirable. We are born innocent and pure and with a desire to make correct choices. But as we move through childhood and adolescence and become contaminated by influences of the world, we learn to compromise, and thereby become fallen.

Nor do evil intentions confine themselves to the physical body. They arise in the heart and mind and spirit, and then bodies become victims of compromise. In its mortal state, physical bodies are subject to a variety of frailties and imperfections. Still, normal sexual drives and feelings are not in this category. God gave us sexuality and commanded us to use this power and process within the bonds of marriage, for it is the best institution for housing all the needs of a man and a woman.

To summarize, it is important to seriously consider intimacy in marriage because it is so crucial to the success of marriage. Too many marriages have been wrecked on the treacherous rocks of ignorance and illicit sexual behavior. Proper sexual intimacy, on the other hand, stands alone in its ability to facilitate oneness.

It is tragic that, despite the crucial nature of this part of marriage, many parents do not educate and equip their children with correct information regarding sexuality. Too many turn their heads away, hoping that in some magical way their children will gather and assimilate this information correctly. Sex Education classes at school give children the basics, but parents need to fill in the blanks with love and understanding.

The approach of letting "the village do it" inadvertently invites teenagers to educate themselves. At best, this education is likely to be incomplete. In addition, many have brought misconceptions from youth to marriage, so they retain an incorrect or inadequate perspective of physical intimacy.

The Sexual Union

Several years ago when Brent began his doctoral studies in the area of marriage and family therapy, he was introduced to the writings of Helen Singer Kaplan, M.D., Ph.D., professor of psychiatry and founder and director of the Human Sexuality Program at New York Hospital-Cornell Medical Center. As both a physician and a psychiatrist, she is eminently qualified to teach about the sexual union.

This Kaplan has done, writing two professional texts, the first of which was titled *The New Sex Therapy*. While this book is written for the professional marriage counselor, it provides some basic and valuable information. If you are contemplating marriage in the near future, or if you've been married for some time, sharing this knowledge of the sexual response cycle can be helpful to you.

The Cycle of Sexual Intimacy

Dr. Kaplan divides the male and the female sexual response into four successive stages: excitement, plateau, orgasm, and resolution. (See *The New Sex Therapy*, pp. 7-33.) Each person experiences physiological, and emotional changes in each of these four stages, as follows:

The Excitement Stage

Most of the time we are not experiencing sexual feelings. Our minds are occupied with other things such as driving the car, golfing, studying, working, eating, cleaning house, caring for the children, taking care of civic responsibilities, and so forth. Still, every once in a while something happens within us that creates a slight sexual feeling. We may be holding hands at a special moment, or we may touch each other in just the right way, or we may have a prearranged signal that tells our partner we are longing to share our feelings of love in a physical way.

Physiologically, this phase is characterized by the onset of erotic feelings, accompanied by a physical response in men and lubrication in women. In addition, the woman's body changes and enlarges to allow a union to take place.

One of the greatest mishaps in new marriages occurs when a husband, without understanding the need for his bride's physical preparation, expects immediate consummation, thus leaving his companion unsatisfied and emotionally and physically unable to respond. When this usually painful cycle repeats itself often enough, the wife will often feel that she is an object rather than a participant. Thus the grounds for disenchantment are unknowingly laid.

This tragic beginning to intimacy is usually due to the different sexual scripts that we bring with us into marriage. We have a preconceived idea of how we want to respond to these feelings of excitement, or intense interest, and our idea or script does not match what our spouse thinks should take place.

In talking about the need for couples to understand and share their preconceived notions, noted therapist, Dr. Carlfred Broderick, states:

> When a couple feels dissatisfied with (the sexual) part of the relationship, it is extremely helpful to share their sexual scripts with each other. Many couples find it difficult to do this because one or both may view sex as so sacred or so private or so shameful that it is very uncomfortable to discuss in any detail.

Nevertheless, it is my experience that a sharing of sexual scripts can provide the awareness needed to solve many perplexing problems in this area. It is like turning on a light in a dark room so that one can see more clearly what the real obstacles to shared satisfaction might be. (*Couples*, Simon & Schuster, Inc., New York, 1987, p. 140.)

One couple shares the following about setting the right mood for physical intimacy:

The sexual part of our life is very different at different times. At times it has been a spiritual experience. When we have been trying to conceive a child we have sometimes felt a kinship with God and have felt that our sexual interaction was almost a heavenly process. We've felt like we were assisting God in the creation process, and it has been a spiritual feeling that initiates our desire to be intimate with each other.

At other times our intimacy has been a means of sustaining and support. When one of us is low, we love to be close and to be touching with each other. Sometimes we'll snuggle up and lay close to each other for a while, and it is a rejuvenating feeling which may or may not lead to a full expression of our love.

There are other times when our desire for closeness has been born of romantic notions. We sometimes decide days before to have a night of romance, and we make a date with each other. As that special time arrives, we may get dressed up and go to dinner, or have a special meal or dessert at home, listen to some of our favorite music, and eventually find ourselves sharing love.

We have also found that the intimate part of our marriage is precious after there has been a problem or difficulty between us. When we have had a serious disagreement or a problem between us that has brought tears and hurt and sadness, we find that the concluding act of getting over the problem is to initiate lovemaking as a healing experience. Somehow this helps us

get close together again, and this has become sort of a signal
to both of us that there is no discomfort between us.

Our society has taught that the husband is to be the aggressor, the one who makes the initial advance toward sexual intimacy. From our experience, this is a false and chauvinistic notion. When the wife assumes the aggressor role and shows interest, it is rewarding to both.

If a wife or a husband is romantic and shows that they are seeking affection early in the day, those desires and feelings build for both partners until evening when the house is quiet and those feelings can be adequately expressed. Anticipation adds fire and emotion to this vital stage.

Another couple adds:

I remember one time when we were going on a trip together.
We flew to New York, and toward the end of the flight we found
ourselves holding hands and squeezing each other in ways that
signaled that we were getting interested in expressing our love.
We then had to wait for a bus ride to the hotel, and both of us
were so excited that we could hardly stand it. As soon as we
could get checked in, we had a passionate and rewarding evening
together.

In considering this first stage of excitement, whatever the initial trigger mechanism for romantic expressions, this stage is characterized by the onset of erotic feelings for one's partner.

Like any other emotion, sexual excitement begins as a small feeling. Also, like many other emotions, this feeling can grow and expand until it becomes very intense, compelling and consuming. If you are presently in a healthy, growing marriage, you will appreciate that these feelings are natural for both you and your spouse, and that they contribute to the depth and breadth of your relationship.

In summarizing the excitement or sexual arousal stage, the important thing to remember is that each partner must trust in order to proceed with an expression of intimacy. You've heard the old saying that "you get more with sugar than you do with vinegar." Sugar, or acts of kindness, create a deep and powerful trust between a husband and wife, and this trust is developed by understanding each other's scripts, or each other's expectations, of this most intimate expression of love.

The Plateau Stage

When a couple is adequately aroused, and an intimate expression of love has commenced, a plateau period takes place. Couples usually experience more and more excitement until gradually they reach this plateau, which is accompanied by both partners beginning to focus on this intimate expression while leaving the cares of the world behind. They find themselves experiencing a continual feeling of intense elation and enjoyment.

During plateau, the local physical response is at its peak for both the husband and the wife. While this is true, it is important to understand that there is a very distinct difference in the way the husband and the wife normally respond in the excitement and plateau stages. The man usually moves through the excitement phase more quickly than does the woman. When this occurs he is physiologically and emotionally ready to consummate the sexual act before she is.

If the couple tries to complete the sexual union at this time, it can create several problems. The wife may not be adequately lubricated and subsequently experience discomfort and even pain. In addition, she may not be emotionally ready to proceed, and may therefore resent her husband's attempts to prematurely effect the union. This is a prime example of the disparity in sexual scripts. It wouldn't take too many repetitions of this theme for a mutual resentment and frustration to be built up about this most crucial and sacred moment in marriage.

Even if you, as a couple, feel that you understand each other's scripts and that you believe you have great similarity in sexual role expectations, it would be good to periodically discuss your patterns of interacting. As couples move through the various stages of love, their sexual expectations and abilities change; and so by doing this you will learn to respond more adequately to the needs of your spouse. You will continue to love each other in ways that will allow you to move through the natural cycle of becoming aroused and excited, thus preparing your mind, your body, your emotions, and your spirit for the moment of sharing love.

One woman shares her perceptions about this stage:

"Tender touch is a very important part of this plateau stage of making love. It is the caressing and touching and trying to please your partner that gives you a warm and responsive feeling. One who is thinking of his or her own needs, or who is spectatoring by examining the experience as an outsider, cannot adequately help their partner achieve satisfaction. On the other hand, one who is trying to please their partner, in an unselfish manner, will receive satisfaction back."

Brent says, "If there is one observation I have made during the past two decades of marital counseling, it is that husbands become too concerned with the act of lovemaking, while ignoring the needs of their wife. When this happens, apprehensions and inhibitions build up in both. I honestly believe that if a woman is treated tenderly and shown concern for her satisfaction, she will desire expressions of intimacy every bit as much as does her husband. Women are emotional creatures, and when a husband positively responds to the emotional needs of his companion, very fulfilling moments of intimacy take place."

When a man is experiencing the act of love, his mind usually has single vision and he concentrates fully on what is transpiring. A woman, on the other hand, often has mental distractions. She may be thinking of other things such as wondering if someone remembered to close the garage door, or if the teens are home from the dance.

The right romantic setting is very important so the couple can forget the world and be totally, mentally caught up in the sharing experiencing with each other. All master bedrooms, in homes where

71

children reside, should have a door with a lock on them. A busy home with family members coming and going at all hours of the day and night make it hard for a couple to find a few minutes together alone. You need to orchestrate romantic time!

The plateau stage can also be portrayed as a time to verbalize one's feelings toward their spouse.

As one husband suggests:

Silence during lovemaking can be like a wall of ice. I love it when my wife and I talk to each other when we are being intimate. I often hear my wife's words, "I love how you love me." She has told me time and again how she likes to hear me describe how I feel toward her, and what I am experiencing. I also ask her, "What pleases you most?" True fulfillment is reaching out to our partner and trying to fulfill their needs. Often a sweet "Thank you for loving me" is the beautiful conclusion to our expression.

We are now ready to discuss the emotion-filled third phase of sexual intimacy.

The Orgasmic Stage

The orgasmic stage, or culminating moment, is usually the shortest of the four stages of sharing love and seldom lasts more than a few seconds. It is the brief period when the peak of sexual excitement occurs and creates a moment of intense feeling of love and expressions of tender affection for the spouse.

Physiologically, the moment of orgasm has three components for the husband: (a) semi-involuntary muscular contractions in the entire abdominal area; (b) extremely intense and pleasant sensations; and © an ejaculation of semen containing up to 50,000 life-producing chromosomes called spermatozoa.

The moment of climax for the wife has two physiological components: (a) a series of semi-involuntary muscular contractions similar to the husband's; and (b) the same type of intense and

72

pleasant sensations. Her vaginal muscles contract and give a sudden feeling similar to a sneeze.

While there are many myths about men and women desiring and needing to achieve simultaneous and mutual orgasm, when a couple knows and understands each other's sexual scripts, they can provide total fulfillment for each other. When they seek to understand each other's feelings and needs (as well as their comfort zones), and when there is mutual trust and respect, the peak physical response becomes effortless and even secondary. The important thing is that couples talk and verbalize their needs and expectations.

A woman does not always need to experience orgasm in order to achieve total fulfillment. Nor does her husband. In fact, as man ages, his regenerative or refractory period (the amount of time which must elapse between orgasmic experiences) increases as well. On the other hand, a woman's ability for peak physical response increases as she passes through her twenties and thirties. A man's ability to perform peaks at the conclusion of his teen years. A love-making session can end without one or both partners achieving orgasm and not create great frustration if there is understanding.

As a couple ages, each partner should be sensitive to each other's physiological abilities and limitations. When a person understands the needs and abilities of his or her partner, and is then sensitive to those needs, the physical act becomes an expression of love rather than a moment of selfish pleasure-seeking. The key to fulfillment is providing emotional gratification during this intimate exchange, while allowing the physiological effects to become secondary to the emotional needs of each partner.

And now for the vital final stage in the sexual response cycle.

The Resolution Stage

Once emotional and/or physical orgasm takes place, a couple concludes the sexual embrace with a period of gradual reduction in sexual and emotional excitement.

During this stage, the resolution for the husband is involuntary and begins to occur within a few seconds after orgasm. The entire

73

resolution phase for him may be over in a period as short as ten to thirty seconds. He then enters a period of sexual satiation and is unable to physically respond for a period of time.

For a woman, the resolution stage lasts longer than for her husband. It is during this stage that she will experience what is commonly referred to as the afterglow. Her interest in being physically close and romantic may take fifteen to thirty minutes to subside. It is important that couples respond with understanding, to this natural difference between the husband and wife during the resolution stage. An abrupt ending on the part of the husband, such as turning on the television or insensitively rolling over and going to sleep, can undo much of the bonding that has just occurred during the sexual union.

If it is ignored, it can cause resentment and do ultimate damage to the perceived fulfillment of each partner.

One woman shares:

> *Much has happened through the years in my husband's understanding my needs and then responding to them. This is especially true as we conclude a session of intimate lovemaking. I have particularly appreciated the empathy my husband shows to my needs, and the discovery we have made to use these concluding moments of intimacy as a time to share feelings and needs we may have at that time. Lying in each other's arms at that time has given an added dimension to our oneness with each other.*

We have discovered that the concluding stage of sharing love can be one of the most fulfilling moments of intimacy. It can become a time when feelings are shared verbally, where empathetic conversation can take place as one partner seeks to understand how his or her spouse is feeling, and where mutual interests can be discussed.

Dealing with Issues and Setbacks

> *Love is not love which alters when it alteration finds.*
> **Shakespeare**

The following experiences come from two couples who confided in us. The first of these was a young man and woman who had recently become engaged and were full of hope and expectations. We found that the young woman was anxious about their approaching marriage. She had been fed inaccurate and unfortunate information from her mother regarding the role of intimacy in marriage. Consequently, whenever this couples' wedding date would draw near, she would postpone the date in fear of what the wedding night might bring.

The four of us visited late into the evening, and before long we became insignificant observers as this couple talked openly with each other. Fortunately for this young woman, her fiancé was wise beyond his years, and because he showed great concern for her and empathy about the situation, her fears began to dissipate. The true magic of that evening became evident as the young woman realized, for the first time, that her fiancé was concerned more about her emotional comfort zone than about his own expectations of their wedding night.

Once this young man displayed such sensitivity, the couple proceeded toward their date with destiny. This time their wedding date was kept, and they now seem to be safely and securely launched into their own marriage orbit. There is power in getting started on the right foot. Because fears and expectations were brought out in the open, and then discussed, this couple avoided problems that seemed inevitable.

The story of the second couple is not as happy. This husband and wife wed almost forty years ago. Unlike the first couple, they

75

married with little or no discussion about perceptions and expectations of sexual intimacy in their relationship.

Unfortunately, as their marriage began the new husband showed little consideration and sensitivity toward his bride's needs and feelings. The result was all too common. During ensuing weeks and months this young woman developed increasing resentment toward her husband for the way he approached their brief moments of what she began to call mechanical intimacy.

Time passed, and after having several children this lonely and unfulfilled wife terminated any sexual activity with her husband. In her mind she did this out of survival, and she resolved to never allow her husband near her again. Her husband subsequently sought gratification outside their marriage, and he now finds himself without a companion and family.

This second scenario is, tragically, too often repeated. There are two recurring reasons for this downward spiraling trend. First and foremost is the lack of understanding and preparation on the part of both partners prior to their wedding date. Second, and equally as tragic, is the courtship born of selfishness, a courtship where making out and physical gratification dominate the pre-wedding relationship. This type of behavior tends to accelerate into even greater selfishness after marriage vows are made. The physical part of the relationship is only one facet of the total. It is just one spoke of the wheel. To be well-rounded, all facets need to have attention.

Starting Over—To Share Love, Rather Than Merely "Have Sex"

As difficult as such circumstances and patterns are, it is possible to reverse this trend—even after years of marriage. If you and your partner are discouraged and bogged down because of unfulfilling moments of intimacy, we recommend that you make preparations to begin to change.

Simply talk through issues, and put the intimate part of your marriage on hold. Indicate to each other that you will re-consummate your marriage vows after you have determined to share moments of intimacy on a more elevated basis. That is, agree that from this moment you will not relegate the sacred intimate expression of lovemaking to simply having sex. Instead, promise that you will prepare to always share love. "Having sex" in and of itself can be a selfish experience, one that too often doesn't lead to growth and bonding. On the other hand, expressing love can become one of the most unifying experiences a couple can experience.

After you have allowed the tension and uncomfortable habits of surrounding intimacy to dissipate and leave your bedroom, prepare for your renewal moment by getting away from the children and having a second honeymoon. An alternative is to arrange for your children to visit their grandparents or friends while you stay home alone and rediscover your love for each other.

Finally, remember that when considering this most personal part of marriage, the word *sacred* is paramount. Friends and family members have no right to information about this part of your relationship. The only time it may be appropriate to share details of such a personal nature is if you determine to seek guidance from the appropriate ecclesiastical leader and/or professional counselor.

CONCLUSION

The amount of satisfaction a couple experiences in sexual intimacy is directly related to the overall satisfaction they have with their marriage. Physical intimacy is the single most predictive barometer of satisfaction a couple has in their marriage.

Our intent in this chapter has been threefold: first, to discuss how this beautiful and profound facet of intimacy should be regarded—that is, within the sacred framework God has ordained. Second, to provide a detailed statement about the physical process and punctuation marks of lovemaking; and third, to explore the foundation of a healthy, satisfying physical relationship.

With the prelude of verbal and nonverbal intimacy as a foundation, and now with an understanding of the facilitative nature of physical or sexual intimacy, it is time to examine the emotional element of intimacy.

7
Emotional Intimacy

Love gives itself—it is not bought.
Longfellow

The Sustaining Nourishment of Marriage

As important as physical intimacy is in marriage, emotional intimacy—the ability to completely trust and give yourself to someone else emotionally—is even more critical. Emotional intimacy can sustain couples, and in fact any meaningful relationship, if need be, through the most trying of circumstances and across great distances.

Learning to identify and understand emotions is a lifelong quest. Emotions are fragile, spontaneous, and unpredictable. Even so, those who learn how to be close emotionally will find that an added dimension of bonding or oneness takes place.

The goal of this chapter is to explore three central themes: emotional health, emotional honesty, and emotional maturity.

Partners who learn to deal successfully with their emotions in each of these areas are well on their way to complete intimacy and oneness in their marriage.

Several years ago, on a Friday evening, we cornered our eleven-year-old daughter Jennifer and asked her to baby-sit while we went to the movies. She wasn't thrilled with the prospect of spending a weekend night tending her three younger brothers and younger sister, but she knew that her four elder brothers were nowhere to be found and that she was elected by default. She hesitantly accepted.

It was our night out, and we were anxious to see the movie our eldest son had recommended—*Willow*.

We weren't disappointed in the movie. *Willow* is a story of adventure, but even more it was the story of a man who loved his wife and two children enough to leave them so that he could ultimately provide safety for them. At the conclusion of the story, when the family was reunited, we were both teary-eyed.

As we ordered dinner after the movie, we talked about how kind this husband and wife were to each other. That movie prepared us emotionally to enjoy the remainder of the evening together. It helped us be open with each other, and it set the mood for gentle, sensitive interchange.

In reflecting upon our need as people to become `one', we will consider the two different types of love described in Brent's doctoral studies. The first, articulated by a scholar named Winch, states: *"We love those who satisfy our needs."* A differing orientation to love is shared by a family scholar named Prescott: *"We satisfy the needs of those we love."*

The first definition is obviously a selfish one and, in fact, is in direct contrast to the very word *love*. The second definition, however, reflects a more giving, Christlike kind of love and exhibits emotional maturity.

Consider this verse by an unidentified author:

> *I suppose it was something you said*
> *That caused me to tighten*
> *And pull away.*

And when you asked, "What is it?"
I of course said, "Nothing."
Whenever I say "Nothing,"
You may be certain there is something.

That little word *nothing* is a sure signal that something needs to be shared.

Margaret states: "I love flowers! Roses are my very most favorite flowers. Every time I see a rose I think of how much marriage is like a rose. Let us compare the emotional state of marriage to a budding rose. If the bud is kept in a cool room without proper light, it will remain tightly closed and show only two or three of its petals. But if the bud has ample light, water, and warmth, it will blossom in a natural way. Only in full bloom can the full beauty of the rose and all its petals be seen. A bud cannot be forced open without damaging its delicate petals. Thus, the process of blooming has to occur naturally and spontaneously.

"The rose is much like a marriage relationship. Where there is a fear of being ridiculed, or being put down, the cool atmosphere may prevent our companion from opening up and sharing honest feelings. But when there is an atmosphere of warmth and trust, it is much easier and less risky to open up and share emotions. This kind of emotional interchange cannot be forced. But it will happen naturally when the climate is right.

"As marriage partners we can provide the greenhouse atmosphere in our home so that our companion will truly blossom emotionally."

One couple gives this example of being emotionally honest with each other:

Sometimes one of us wants to make love and the other doesn't. The one who doesn't may be too tired or may just not be interested. For years in our marriage we struggled with how to "say no" in ways that didn't make the other person feel badly. When that is the case, one thing we try to do is make a date for a later time. We have found this helps the one who was interested to be patient and to not feel unloved or rejected.

Benevolent Blindness and Discriminatory Deafness

Several years ago, while Brent was co-authoring a marriage strengthening program with his colleagues, Wesley Burr and Terry Baker, they developed a concept that Brent claims is one of the few original ideas he has ever had. Even so, he quickly acknowledges that Wes first articulated the concept, but that he and Terry helped inspire its discovery. The concept is a simple yet powerful one: *benevolent blindness.*

Brent remembers the day they first centered on this notion. "We talked about the far-reaching implications this idea could have. Terry realized that, while he hadn't had a label for it, his wife, Patti, had been practicing benevolent blindness for years. 'In fact,' he admitted, 'if she hadn't, I'm sure our marriage would have ended long ago.'"

Stated simply, benevolent blindness is the idea that married couples should always be benevolently blind to each other's imperfections.

Brent continues: "One of the things I have appreciated most about Margaret is that she, like Patti, has nearly perfected this notion. She keeps her eyes half closed to my imperfections (leaving them slightly open so that she can see to pick up my dirty socks, if I have forgotten to put them into the hamper, and so forth). And taking things a step further, she doesn't make me pay for these imperfections, whatever they might be. Believe me, her benevolent approach is like magic and works miracles in our marriage."

It has been said that we should marry someone who inspires us to grow and improve *at our own choice.* If you are the partner who is practicing "long-suffering" (something that applies to each of us at different times in our marriages), try quietly encouraging, not nagging, and then pray that your partner will become sensitive to the need to improve.

On one occasion we visited with some friends about the concept of benevolent blindness, and the woman, who is very bright and articulate, quipped: "There is another concept couples should incorporate, and that is what I call *discriminatory deafness*. My husband and I have learned that when one of us speaks an unkind word (whether the comment was intentional or not), we try not to take what is said personally. We have often talked of our going deaf to an inappropriately expressed thought or emotion, and we feel it has saved us from a great deal of conflict."

None of us will make it on this journey called matrimony without having our feelings hurt, or, on the other hand, without hurting our companion's feelings.

Benevolent blindness and discriminatory deafness, when practiced by both partners simultaneously, can have incredible impact on the quality and satisfaction of the relationship.

Though Problems May Arise

As mentioned earlier, there are times for all couples when situations arise that cause emotional pain or discomfort for one or both partners. This is called life. It would be nothing short of impossible for two people from different backgrounds, and therefore different expectations, to travel the road of life without running into obstacles, roadblocks and hazards that create frustration and pain.

While this isn't a startling revelation, unfortunately some couples become resigned to their pain and simply decide to stick it out. They do this because (a) they have made a promise to stay married, (b) they don't want to admit social failure, or (c) they determine to remain in an unsatisfactory relationship because of the children.

Reflective Retrenching

Is it reasonable to believe that divorce and tolerance are the only two solutions to a troubled relationship? No, there is another alternative. We call this option *reflective retrenching*. This is the process of getting away from the children for an hour, a day, a weekend, or even longer, if necessary. Once away, a husband and wife are free to consider what is blocking the relationship, what barriers may be inhibiting the relationship, or what is causing the pain-ridden emotions that either or both partners may be experiencing. It is a time to get to the root of the problem without blaming or manipulating each other, and then determining how to remedy the situation.

We have identified several barriers to emotional intimacy that seem to reoccur in marriages.

Perhaps you are at your wit's end. You may even be contemplating a divorce. Or, maybe your marriage is intact, but you just don't feel a closeness to your partner anymore. Whatever the reason for your despair, the following information may help you reverse your collision course and begin your marriage anew.

Barriers to Emotional Intimacy

Barrier Number One

Your marriage has become a flat tire. All of the "air" has gone out of it, and moving forward seems impossible. You feel very discouraged about your marriage and are perhaps even in a state of total despair. There doesn't seem to be much hope.

We suggest to those of you to whom this sounds all too familiar that where there was once air, air can rise again. We honestly believe what was stated at the beginning of this book; that if two people love each other when they marry (in other words, there is lots of air), and *if they both remain true to their shared values*, that marriage need never end in divorce.

You can begin to re-inflate your marital tire by acting as though there is still oxygen in your marriage. Act as though emotions and feelings of love exist. This cannot be done with a critical eye, but must be done with 100 percent effort on both parts—and, of course, with benevolent blindness. This is not to say that you won't have a bad day once in a while. Rekindling feelings of love is a process, not an event or a commitment. But the commitment to act as though you feel the emotions you no doubt felt during courtship will be a beginning. By being blind to the weaknesses of your spouse, or in your relationship, it is possible to recapture that which was once beautiful and alive.

Deutch's Law of Reciprocity

Professional counselors and marriage advisors refer to a principle know as *Deutch's Law*. Applied to marriage, it is: "The more we act in a certain way, the more our partner will act in that same way."

This law has two components: the ripple effect and the restoration effect. The ripple effect is stated above. The restoration effect comes into play when those around us model our good behavior, thus reinforcing our actions and encouraging us to perpetuate the same behavior.

The more one partner displays loving behavior (even though that behavior may at first seem awkward and contrived), the more the other partner responds by acting in the same way. This can only cause an escalation of loving emotions and loving events in the marriage.

Barrier Number Two

The second barrier occurs when a person does not feel accepted by his or her partner (which is emotional rejection), regardless of the love displayed and the loving behavior shared.

A feeling of rejection causes some of the deepest pain a person can experience, and it is not easily dealt with. Too often, when a person rejects his or her partner, it is because of personal selfishness and/or unrighteousness.

Selfishness can destroy even what may have been a strong marriage. Couples who are moving forward in their relationship are those who have learned to put in more than they expect to draw out — an attribute that is admittedly challenging to develop and even harder to maintain. But until a husband and wife agree to throw away the ledger wherein they keep track of every misunderstanding and mistake, a couple must realize that no two people have the same needs for love and that needs can be met in different ways.

Don't make your partner feel guilty when his or her needs are different from yours; neither should you feel rejection when your needs are different than his or hers. Learn to think of your companion—his or her needs, desires, feelings, and so forth—first.

Betrayal in marriage is perhaps the greatest facilitator in breaking up a once harmonious home. If either you or your partner need to confess a violation of your marriage vows, then for your marriage's sake, do it!

One of the basic principles of our society is agency. Even though it is difficult to continue to endure, some individuals sometimes must live with their pain until their spouse decides to excise his or her own pain—usually through confessing and leaving behind former transgressions through whatever means your minister or pastor advises.

Violating marital vows is not the only cause of rejection. This can also occur when a person feels a gradual reduction of feelings of attraction to his or her spouse. This sometimes occurs when the partner's metabolism changes at mid life and extra pounds, chins and inches appear.

We think of two good friends, a husband and wife, who both put on a few pounds and added some inches as they moved through their early fifties. We remember visiting with this man on one occasion. He remarked that it didn't matter to him how heavy his wife was, even though they were walking together each evening and were making an effort to take better care of their bodies. What was important was their acceptance of each other and the way they were.

One friend defines *perfection* as being whoever and whatever his wife is. He applies this definition to all areas of their relationship. What a healthy implementation of benevolent blindness!

Another friend says about her marriage of over twenty years: "In our intimate life, my husband always makes me feel as though I am the most desirable woman ever. He never notices the physical flaws; or if he does, he doesn't mention them. I hope I do the same for him, although he doesn't have many flaws that I have found."

There is much to learn from these couples and from their

approach to their changing circumstances. The reward for each of these individuals is that their companions find great satisfaction and fulfillment in marriage because they do not sense rejection or receive criticism from their spouses.

Barrier Number Three

If the romance starts to leave the marriage, there is a tendency, which is also a trap, for a person to begin to dwell on who their partner *isn't*. The experience of one couple illustrates this point. Margaret begins to tell this story from her perspective:

> Several years ago we were living in Arizona. We lived near a beautiful, older couple who had been married for twenty-seven years. Not long after we had moved into the area, Brent was asked to counsel with this couple, who we'll refer to as James and Dorothy. Although I was unaware of it, they were on the verge of a divorce.
> Brent began to work with them. He tried everything he knew from his training, and nothing seemed to encourage this couple to want to continue as husband and wife. Finally, just before we were to move from the area, Brent got an idea.
> He spent the next several evenings on an oil painting of the religious chapel where this couple had been married just a few years earlier. In the foreground Brent painted a large cactus with a glazed donut on one of the quills. He then had the painting framed, took it to their home, and brazenly hung it on their living room wall. They thanked him for the gift, though Brent was sure he saw Dorothy wince as he put the painting on her wall. Then James saw the donut.
> "What in the world is that?" he exclaimed, pointing directly to the unusual cactus.
> "What does it look like?" Brent countered, enjoying the moment.
> "Looks like a donut to me," Dorothy stated, her brow furrowed.

"You're right, Dorothy," Brent replied. "It is a donut, and I painted it especially for you."

"For me?" Dorothy questioned, pointing to herself.

"It's the least I could do," Brent said, pausing to allow their puzzled expressions to linger. "Dorothy, that donut represents James, as seen from your eyes. Up until now, whenever you have thought of James all you have seen is his 'holes'. You've concentrated on all the things he 'isn't'. From now on, whenever you see that donut, you will be reminded to see who he is. Let's consider just a few things. James has not missed a day's work for over twenty-five years. He has never been unfaithful to you. He is as trustworthy as any man I have known. I really believe that if you begin to dwell on his attributes, rather than on his weaknesses, your marriage fire will rekindle to its original flame."

Four years passed, and we were living where Brent was pursuing his doctoral studies. One Monday evening the doorbell rang. Standing in the doorway were James and Dorothy. No sooner had the door opened than James swooped Dorothy down, planted his lips on hers, and took her breath away in a kiss that lasted for what seemed like hours. After observing this passionate display, we invited them in and learned that, after thirty-two years of marriage, they were taking a second honeymoon.

When asked what had changed things, Dorothy smiled and said, "Why, the donut, of course. It was Brent's crazy donut."

It was hard to tell who was happier, James or Brent.

The moral of the story is clear: Look for donuts rather than the holes. Or, in other words, look for what's *in* your relationship, not what's missing. Cologne and perfume will be purchased in great abundance thereafter.

One woman, after becoming acquainted with the "donut" story, said: "I had a great experience in collecting donuts a few years ago. I got a piece of paper and pen and then began to write down the traits I had grown to love and appreciate in my husband. As it turned out, I filled both sides of the paper. I wrote these traits in my personal journal so that I could save these donuts through time. Then I wrote a love note to my husband and specifically told him what I appreciated about him and why I loved him so much."

We can each go on a donut search, looking for the qualities we appreciate in and love about our mate. When we are intently looking, these qualities become more apparent.

Barrier Number Four

An unresolved negative experience from youth, where either mental or physical abuse occurred, can create barriers to intimacy. It is difficult to understand those adults who betray their trust by abusing children in some fashion. But it happens. And if a person has experienced some form of abuse—emotional, physical, and so forth—during childhood, it is possible for that person to later experience a kind of emotional paralysis during marriage and find it difficult to open up and trust another person in marriage, a setting that demands trust.

One friend explains:

I don't know when dad began to abuse two of us, but we each carried our own secret into our own marriages. From the time we were little, dad would tuck us into bed. When the lights were out, he would physically abuse us, all the time whispering that we could never tell. And we didn't tell. That is, not until the two of us talked one day and shared the distrust we both felt in our intimate expressions that we had for our husbands. I told my sister that I was repulsed by any man's touch, and the conversation went from there.

This was difficult for us to deal with, but we both went back to our husbands and told all. We lived in the same area, and so the next Sunday the four of us visited our minister and told him. Unfortunately, Dad had died two years earlier, but still we prayed for strength to forgive him.

One of the happiest days for our family took place a year

later. After getting rid of all the anger and betrayal, and after having professional counseling for our own marriages, we spent a very special "forgiving" evening together. We each have a sense of peace now, and we are now able to open up and trust in our own marriages. It has been a long road, but for us it has been worth every minute of it.

If you find yourself inhibited in and perhaps even blocking out emotional as well as physical intimacy, perhaps these feelings stem from experiences you had during childhood. Abuse comes in various forms—physical, mental, and emotional. All leave their mark.

If this is the case, go to your religious leader and rid yourself of this guilt. Persons who live with the memory of being sexually abused as a child, for example, usually feel at least partially responsible and guilty about the experience. Some carry the guilt for years because they didn't know how to stop it once the abusive behavior began.

If someone abused you, you will be doing that individual a favor by also going to their appropriate ecclesiastical leader and by sharing the misdeed with that religious steward.

While this could be the most difficult decision you will ever make, it is the only way for you to heal and grow, and it is also the only way for the individual concerned to be given the opportunity to repent and move ahead with life.

The payoff for you will be the removal of hatred and anger that you have probably been carrying for years. You will begin to see the person who abused you as having a form of cancer rather than as someone who is evil. The ultimate payoff, of course, will be the enhanced nature of your own marriage relationship.

Barrier Number Five

Another barrier to intimacy can stem from a feeling of distrust from previous inappropriate expectations and/or behavior on the part of your spouse.

Couples often wonder just what is appropriate in terms of the way they express love to each other. The answer is really quite simple. It requires establishing sexual boundaries—a value-laden foundation—then being true to that foundation.

One of the greatest mistakes individuals make, especially in the area of physical intimacy in marriage, is a year-in and year-out toleration of behavior that is inappropriate or undesirable. If you are unable to convince your partner that you are uncomfortable with part of your intimate moments, you should feel free to visit either a therapist, or your ecclesiastical leader.

When we first married, we pledged to totally respect the feelings and wishes of each other. That commitment has governed the way we interact with each other physically. Your partner does not own you, nor does he or she have the option of taking you somewhere you don't want to go. Love cannot blossom if it is not built upon the foundation of trust and mutual respect.

Barrier Number Six

Closely related to barrier number five, this barrier involves a propensity, usually on the part of the husband, to be involved in pornography. In the age of Internet pornography this is especially accessible and evasive. This problem is almost always a leftover from indulgent behavior as a teenager and is extremely destructive—both to the mental wholeness of the individual as well as to the intimacy of the couple.

Pornography can have stifling effects on a marriage relationship. The person so addicted obtains unreal expectations of intimacy in general and of his partner specifically. Pornography addiction can ruin marriage. It's as simple, yet as deadly, as that.

If you, or your partner, suffer from the illness of addiction to pornography, either visit immediately with your ecclesiastical leader, or seek professional help. There are those who claim that such activity actually enhances marital intimacy. But that is a lie, and is a destructive relationship tool of the first order!

True intimacy will never take place while one of the partners is involved in pornography. Pornography addiction is just that—an addiction every bit as debilitating as some forms of drug abuse. If professional counseling is required, don't hesitate to seek it.

As a caution to the spouse of one involved in pornography, it is essential to know that the use of such literature [or visual images on the Internet] can lead to a real illness. A supportive, noncritical spouse can be of great assistance in helping someone remove this cancer from their system.

Barrier Number Seven

Another barrier that can impede the progress of intimacy is the feeling that the relationship is not equal—that one partner does most of the giving, while the other does most of the taking.

Brent explains: "I truly think that we men are the weaker sex. We are more inclined to selfishness and to false pride, and we seem to develop the notion that equality is merely a buzz word not really to be taken seriously."

Margaret gives her viewpoint: "Marriage is not equal. I honestly believe that women do have the most difficult roles. That is perhaps why Brent feels we are not the weaker sex—we simply don't take time to relax or even rest when we are ill. Being a wife and mother means someone always needs you, and you want to be there for them. I think that most women understand our differentness and the consuming nature of our tasks. I also think that the thing we value most is *knowing* that our husbands are sensitive to our needs and that they make an effort to lend their support whenever possible, even though their involvement with home and children will probably never equal that of our own."

Someone once said that you cannot tie a knot in a fifty-fifty relationship, and we have found this to be true. While we do not keep score with who does what for whom, we are both aware of trying to meet the needs of the other. Couples who do not make this discovery ultimately find themselves in the rocky and murky grounds of divorce.

There are different seasons in each of our lives. One partner may carry a greater load, from time to time, in the relationship.

We have often joked about titling one of the chapters of this book "Equally Yoked or Forever Choked." We haven't, though, because we know that unless a couple develops equality in their relationship the choking will finally stop—either through death, or on the divorce courthouse steps.

We have each been reared differently and have had different role models. As a result, each of us must be willing to learn, to look, and to listen to each other's ways. We then need to work together to form our own working models that are equally fulfilling to each of us.

Barrier Number Eight

A barrier develops when we maintain a marriage on a superficial, exchange basis. Too many couples who are struggling to survive keep score and give only when they receive. In addition, some individuals perform loving acts for their partner simply to prove they are better, or to store up points to be reserved for the next disagreement.

The partners who limit their relationship to an exchange of this nature never experience altruistic acts of love. They never allow charitable acts to surface, and so their relationship does not deepen and take root in the fertile soil of charity, empathy, and love.

The following demonstrates this point:

Has our marriage ever changed! Several years ago, when I was on the verge of leaving my wife and our three beautiful children, we decided to get away for the weekend and make the decision once and for all what our future would be.

We arranged for a baby-sitter, spent several silent hours driving to who-knows-where, and finally stopped for the night. Our dinner at the restaurant was likewise silent, with each of us thinking about how poorly our companion treated the other in our marriage.

When we got to our room, we sat down around a table and

*in the next four hours we experienced most, if not all, of the
emotions known to man. We learned more about each other,
and the way we had treated each other, than either of us had
previously known.*

*The bottom-line came when I asked my wife why she always
had a string attached to our being intimate. She surprised me
when she said that her string was her only defense, that she
thought I wasn't really concerned about her as a woman, but
just someone to be with. We then talked about how we were
always having to get something in order to give something.
And finally, we both decided to change. At that moment we
slipped to our knees, vowed to not keep score with each other
again, and resolved to make our marriage work.*

*And it has worked. We are now totally immersed in each
other's love, and we get a very queasy feeling whenever we
think of how close we came to losing each other and our
family.*

Barrier Number Nine

Sometimes dutiful wives strive to be such super women that
they rob the husband of equal status in the home, thus causing the
husband to become emotionally paralyzed in the relationship.

Male paralysis sets in when a husband is so doted on that he
feels unwelcome to participate in the home life. For instance, the
wife sees to it that her husband always comes home to a clean house
and delicious meals. The children are under control, and she always
manages to greet her husband with a big smile and a passionate kiss.

We're not suggesting that the woman should not make her
husband's pathway bright when he returns from work each evening.
What we are suggesting is that when a woman successfully plays the
role of the perfect homemaker, resentment can build in the
husband's mind as he begins to feel like an intruder, unable to pitch
in and be part of the daily household activities. A man needs to be
needed!

A friend of ours told us about her experience. She supported her husband through law school, worked full-time for years, and yet always saw to it that he had the red carpet treatment when he returned home each day. This unintentional "over-doting" began to grate on him until finally they separated and planned for divorce. Luckily, a short time later they realized what the problems were. They are now back together, with the husband contributing to the Cub Scout activities, the lawn care, and any other activity he has time for.

This woman reflects:

For years I assumed all of the domestic responsibilities, thinking that I was providing the perfect home for my husband. He began to emotionally withdraw, however, until we both found that we had little to share with each other. We both thought our companion had lost their love for us, and so we agreed to a trial separation.

During our separation we discovered that I had actually wedged my husband out of feeling a part of our home. We have a lot of habits to break, but we are now in the process of rediscovering our love for each other.

As an example of how I now treat my husband, I might tactfully (and I hope with the right timing) ask him to put the groceries away after we have been shopping. I have learned to simply say, "Thank you, dear" after he has completed the task rather than saying, "Thank you, dear, for helping me." The "helping me" phrase somehow caused my husband to think he was being asked to do something that was really not his responsibility, and that in fact he was doing me a favor. I now feel more secure because I know my husband cares and loves me because of his efforts, and he feels good about his involvement because I have allowed him to contribute to the relationship. That, to us, is the crux of making a true intimate relationship.

We don't always recognize that being equal is not the same as being the same. A feeling of emotional equality must exist in marriage if that marriage is to last. Even so, men and women are not the same—and complementarity is valid and healthy.

Not long ago Brent was reminded of the words to a Neil Diamond song:

> *She was morning, and I was night time.*
> *I was lonely, in need of someone—*
> *You are the sun, I am the moon,*
> *You are the words, I am the tune—play me.*

While the world is shouting about how men and women are the same, it's nice to hear words that echo truth. A solid marriage relationship is one that is complementary in nature, where the expectations are different for each partner. Both are half a wheel, and by becoming one whole are able to move steadily forward, always discovering new and exciting horizons in their marriage.

CONCLUSION

We don't claim that this listing of "barriers" is all-inclusive. But we hope these concepts may give you guidance in understanding the things that can limit the intimacy you achieve with your partner.

If, after working with your partner, there are issues that you are unable to resolve, we suggest that you contact a professional marriage counselor. Seeking counseling is not an admission of failure, and whether it be for refining your methods of communicating or dealing with severe sexual problems, counselors are equipped to provide valuable and timely assistance. If you feel that you simply can't afford the fees of a counselor, let us suggest that perhaps you can't afford *not* to afford to see one. It could be one of the most significant phone calls you will make.

Emotional intimacy in marriage creates oneness; and being "one" allows intimacy to flow naturally from the foundation of spontaneity. Being in love is not an adequate license for intimacy, but being physically and emotionally intimate, within the bounds of marriage, is a vehicle that leads to knowing and understanding true love.

8
Spiritual Intimacy

> *God has set the type of marriage everywhere throughout the creation. Every creature seeks its perfection in another. The very heavens and earth picture it to us.*   **Luther**

Introduction

Spiritual intimacy is spirit-to-spirit communication that transcends other forms of oneness. It is a union among three partners—a man, a woman, and their God. This union appears most powerfully in the act of procreation, but includes the marvelous bonding and unifying aspects, as well.

Without apology, this book is written from a value system forged in the belief that the highest intimacy includes the Supreme Being. This intimacy supercedes all the other forms, and it can be yours if you so choose.

Spiritual intimacy is the 'Crown Jewel' of relationship oneness, the most treasured gem of all. It gives a taste of heaven here on earth. It's really true that 'Love makes the world go around.' It's the cherry on top, the *summon bonum* of all the facets of intimacy.

Most of the music written over the centuries is dedicated to the power of love, as musicians try to express the unspeakable joys and pains associated with love. Listen closely to the words as you play love songs. Just to name a few: "You're the meaning in my life, you're my inspiration. . . ." "Love and marriage go together like a horse and carriage." "You light up my life. . . ."

The electricity that flies through the air where there is a spiritual connection is like the power that surges when a multi-breaker is switched on. Hearts connect, light increases, and peace abounds.

Each home has a distinct spirit. Those couples who walk the upper path together, create a home wherein the spirit of peace resides. As you know, it is a joy to enter such a home, and to feel the intimacy that partners, and their children, thrive on.

Many Paths to Spiritual Oneness

One woman shares the perspective she and her husband have with respect to faith and marriage:

My husband and I do not belong to a specific religious faith; nor are we Christians like many of our friends. We do believe in God, however, and we pray to Him daily. We've reared our two children to do the same, and while one of them has declared themselves with a particular sect, the other (and their spouse) is not considered any less.

Of greatest importance, our two children are now married and with small families of their own. These children are learning to rely upon God, and to be true to their values.

That's the main thing—having values that include prayer, trust, dialogue about God, and of course treating each other in a way that invites closeness. We couldn't be more unified as a family, and it all began with how my husband and I began our marriage with reliance on a loving, caring God.

This woman and her family do much to offset the lack of moral leadership in today's society. A couple cannot hope to have spiritual intimacy when one, or both, move in and out of the boundaries of behavior they've established as acceptable.

You have seen the pain that hardens the hearts of great people who turn from their partners and families. You have also observed them create convenient rationalizations for their immorality and/or relationship compromises. Such justifications merely gloss over the pain and despair these errant partners have in their hearts.

On the other hand, many couples express spiritual intimacy by feeling that they are 'soul-mates'. These couples protect themselves from outside intrusions, and invest constant time and energy in enlarging the "soul" of their relationship.

A friend named Cheryl enjoys spiritual intimacy with her husband, even several years after his death. She shares: "I look forward to being reunited with Mick someday and having our family all together again."

Cheryl has an unusual story to tell. She met, fell in love, and married Mick, a quadriplegic. Again she relates: "He couldn't even breathe on his own. He couldn't do the things I would have loved doing with my sweetheart. He couldn't play one-on-one basketball or take walks with me, work in the garden or hike the mountain trails. Even so, we felt a spiritual closeness as we had deep discussions, and shared heart-to-heart our testimony and faith in each other and in Christ. Even though we couldn't make things better while he was here, we lived with the hope that there was a better life to come. We dreamed the impossible dream, and now in my hours of loneliness without Mick, I hang on to that dream."

Two Types of Sorrow

When individuals are "caught" violating their marriage vows, they are experiencing one of two types of sorrow. In both instances, there is sadness, and hearts are bleeding.

> *Sorrow for misbehavior, if properly managed and responded to, can lead to new levels of spiritual intimacy in a committed, charactered relationship.*

The first type of sorrow is the sorrow of the "damned." People who have this sadness appear angry with those who reveal their value-betraying behavior. This anger ripples out into all their relationships including extended family and friends. Bitterness weakens the relationship, often to the point of alienation. Self-betrayers will withdraw and refrain from interacting with friends and family. Fear grips their heart, and anger spews out of their mouth. Tempers flare, wounds deepen, and erosion accelerates. Until this person begins to accept responsibility for his actions, then changes his self-inflicting behavior, intimacy cannot hope to exist.

The second type of sorrow—that which invites a restoration of intimacy—is sorrow unto God-like repentance. This person, while privately and/or publically acknowledging his mistake to his partner and their God, resolves to make amends. And then he does.

Regaining trust in a marriage is a process, not an event, and is earned one day at a time. When both partners work together with forgiving hearts, looking forward with hope, not dwelling on past mistakes, vows can be re-made. Such new beginnings breathe life back into a marriage, and can lead to a happy ending.

The Golden and Platinum Rules

Christ, in the Sermon on the Mount, implores us to live the golden rule—that is, to do unto others as we would have them do unto us.

An additional rule, one that has only recently been articulated, is the platinum rule. It states that we should do unto others as we perceive they would like us to do unto them. It is a rule that involves empathy—considering the feelings of those with whom we interact. In marriage, and in all relationships, we would do well to live both of these rules and enjoy the fruits thereof.

Three Measurements for a Happy Marriage

One model couple is Dallin and June Oaks. Oaks is a former member of the Supreme Court in the state where he lives. In her sixties, June recently passed away with cancer. Her death was accompanied by great sadness, for she had made an impact on so many lives. Together, she and her husband exuded a love that was based on a life of loyalty and trust.

In 1989, Oaks wrote a book titled, *Pure In Heart* (Bookcraft, Inc.) In the first pages of this book, he described the three ingredients of the inner man. These include (1) motives, (2) desires, and (3) attitude. This book helps us understand why people in general do what they do (their motives), what they want to do (their desires), and the spirit in which they conduct themselves (their attitude).

As couples, we can look deep down inside and evaluate our own motives, desires and attitude. Couples who govern their actions with integrity are those whose marriages achieve intimacy, thereby withstanding the storms of life.

When people are able to internalize these three qualities, they become *charactered* by authenticating their behavior to each other. They are able to think and live in a manner consistent with their values, and they do so from the inside. . .out. This mastery not only allows joy to exist within the paradigm of charactered intimacy, but eagerly encourages it!

Total Union

Another couple, Jeffrey and Patricia Holland, are friends and colleagues of Dallin and June Oaks. As president of a large privately-held university, Holland spoke to the student body on the subject of intimacy the same year Oaks' *Pure In Heart* was published. The following is an excerpt from that talk:

103

"I would also suggest that human intimacy, that sacred, physical union ordained of God for a married couple, deals with a symbol that demands special sanctity. Such an act of love between a man and a woman is—or certainly was ordained to be—a symbol of total union: union of their hearts, their hopes, their lives, their love, their family, their future, their everything (*On Earth As It Is in Heaven*, Deseret Book Co., 1989).

According to Holland, and true to the theme of this book, total union—and therefore intimacy—is possible between a man and woman. It does demand sanctity, for it is holy. It is elevated to the level of procreating, forming the very breath of life in another human being.

A Deeply Spiritual Beginning

Margaret reflects upon one of our early discoveries: "Though this experience is sacred to us, Brent and I feel it appropriate to relate a moment of our first night as husband and wife. As we prepared to retire, we knelt in prayer so that the Lord could be included in our marriage. We held hands, and Brent offered our first family prayer. My heart swelled as I listened to his words, savoring the memory of our marriage ceremony just hours earlier.

"Brent then said something I wasn't expecting. He prayed for our expressions of intimacy. At that time, the two of us pledged to never abuse the procreative power that was ours, but to elevate our expression to its intended lofty position."

Years have passed since our first prayer, and with their passing have come challenges we could have never anticipated. Ofttimes these have been moments of frustration, resulting from poor communicating. At other times, they have been monumental intrusions as we were forced to steel ourselves against poor decisions we had made. Still, at all times we have remained true to our early vows. Our relationship authenticity has become the glue that has enabled us to ennoble our marriage. Outside distractions have not penetrated our resolve, nor will they in the future.

104

CONCLUSION

The crowning facet of intimacy is spiritual, where true oneness flourishes. The foundations of intimacy, as shared in Part One, as well as the facets of intimacy in Part Three, build upon being intimately in touch with each other's thoughts, emotions, and spirit.

It is our hope, as authors, that by having shared our personal thoughts and impressions—as well as the expressions of friends—you will have increased resolve to build intimacy in your most significant relationships.

It is also our desire that the ideas shared in this book will serve as a springboard to intimate discussions, then growth, for you and your partner. Take every opportunity to develop and cherish intimacy in your life. Correct bad habits, renew your vows, and forgive and forget disquieting moments of the past. Begin anew, treating each other with increased kindness, and with a resolve to serve one other in the highest manner possible. Be your partner's greatest cheerleader, and help them believe in themselves, in you, and in your combined partnership with God.

Finally, we wish you happiness—with every opportunity for treasured closeness. After all, intimacy cherished—and intimacy nourished—is the *real* stuff life is made of!

To order additional product or information such
as books, tapes, videos or speaking engagements,
please contact: www.TheLincolnInstitute.com